WOMEN'S GOLF SHORTS

1,001 HOLE-IN-ONE-LINERS BY AND ABOUT WOMEN IN GOLF

GLENN LIEBMAN

CB
CONTEMPORARY BOOKS

Library of Congress Cataloging-in-Publication Data

Liebman, Glenn.
    Women's golf shorts : 1,001 hole-in-one-liners by and about
women in golf / Glenn Liebman.
        p.   cm.
    ISBN 0-8092-9876-7
    1. Women golfers—Quotations.   2. Golf—Humor.   I. Title.

    GV964.A1 L54 2001
    796.352'082—dc21

                                                    00-60318

Published by Contemporary Books
A division of NTC/Contemporary Publishing Group, Inc.
4255 West Touhy Avenue, Lincolnwood (Chicago), Illinois 60712-1975 U.S.A.
Printed in the United States of America
International Standard Book Number: 0-8092-9876-7

01 02 03 04 05 06 LB 18 17 16 15 14 13 12 11 10 9 8 7 6 5 4 3 2 1

To Samantha and Joy,
thanks for being such a special part of my life

ACKNOWLEDGMENTS

I appreciate all who helped me with this book especially the wonderful people at NTC/Contemporary—John Nolan, Denise Betts, and Nancy Hall.

I have had the honor of writing several one-liner books and had the pleasure of mentioning a lot of people who have meant a great deal to me over the years.

In recent years, through our family reunions, I have again gotten close to many of my relatives. My mother, Frieda, always embedded in me the importance of family. That said, I would like to acknowledge some of my terrific relatives—the Fischls, the Salpeters, the Sadowskis, the Udelsmans, the Weinstocks, and the Metviners. I'm so glad we have gotten back in touch in recent years.

Speaking of relatives, I would like to thank my dad, Bernie. He continues to show me two of life's most important lessons—perseverance and a great sense of humor.

I'd like to thank my wonderful sister-in-law Deb (by mentioning her and dedicating the books to my nieces—I expect extra latkes and pot roast this year) and my brother Bennett—only the best sibling in the history of the world.

Finally, I'd like to thank the two superstars in my life. Thanks to Frankie for making every day a great adventure. He is a great kid who makes me laugh about five hundred times a day. My next book should be Frankie Shorts (Now go to bed, buddy!), and finally thanks to Kathy, for making every day special. You are a wonderful wife, great mother (who doesn't spoil her kid—well, not too much), and my best friend.

INTRODUCTION

In the more than fifty years of the LPGA tour, a lot
of legends have been created—Babe Didrikson,
Mickey Wright, Nancy Lopez, and Karrie Webb, just
to name a few. All you have to do is witness an
LPGA event to capture the greatness of the tour,
but even the most knowledgeable fan was probably
not fully aware of the extent of the greatness of the
characters and the wit of women's golf.

Women's Golf Shorts was designed with one
purpose in mind—to show the lighter side of women
and golf. Behind the steely-eyed competition and
relentless quest for perfection are volumes of humor
and good cheer.

All the foremost women golf humorists are
here. Pick your favorite. We have competitors from
the golf and humor Hall of Fame like Amy Alcott
(on jumping in the water after winning the Dinah
Shore—"I wanted to accept this trophy with dignity,
but I guess that's just not my style") and Joanne

Carner ("You need thirty wins to qualify for the Hall of Fame. It's important to me. Besides, it makes a great obituary.").

Then you have future golf and humor Hall of Famers like Laura Davies (on why Michael Jordan is her sports idol—"I'd like to be able to bet as much as he does.").

And finally, you have humor Hall of Famers like Lori Garbacz (on leading the first round of a tournament—"Usually my friends start looking for me from the bottom up. Tomorrow, they will wonder why they can't find me.") and Kris Tschetter (explaining her popularity with the gallery—"When you go in the rough as much as I do, there's people there to talk to.").

Whatever Hall of Fame you support, I think you will agree that the women of golf provide many great quotes for every fan—more than 1,000 of them!

"Why should I be sitting in a lab cutting up a frog when I wanted to be out on a fairway?"

> *Amy Alcott, on declining a scholarship to Dartmouth*

"Too bad ASU couldn't just give me a degree in golf."

> *Danielle Ammaccapane, on attending Arizona State University for four years but not getting a degree*

"Betsy studied and played golf. I played golf, partied, and studied a little."

> *Beth Daniel, on herself and Betsy King, who both went to Furman at the same time*

"I have the best of both worlds. I'm a Florida State football fan and a Kentucky basketball fan."

> *Nancy Scranton, on attending Florida State and then transferring to Kentucky*

"Shakespeare isn't doing too much in my life right now."

> LaRee Sugg, LPGA pro, on
> majoring in English in college

"I think she had an extra uniform."

> Karen Weiss, LPGA pro, on making
> her college golf team even though the
> coach was not impressed

ACT YOUR AGE

"Way to go, you old hag."

> Amy Alcott, at age 40, joking with
> 42-year-old Hollis Stacy

"When I was young, I was rebellious and hungry. I don't consider myself rebellious, but I'm still hungry."

> Amy Alcott, at age 35

"By then I'll be 74, just two over par."

> Patty Berg, at age 72, after being
> told it would take two years to
> recover from back surgery

"I'm one of the 20-something players, but I feel like I'm about 50."

> *Brandie Burton, on her many injuries*
> *at age 26*

"I idolized her as a little tyke."

> *Brandie Burton, at age 28, on losing*
> *to 44-year-old Betsy King*

"Oh, how I would love to be 16 again. Then again, I would also love to be 58 again."

> *JoAnne Carner, at age 61*

"They used to say to me, when you're 35 you'll be through. . . . At 45, they were still talking. Then they finally quit."

> *JoAnne Carner, on being competitive*
> *in her 50s*

"Two over-50 players against players in their 20s and 30s. I think that's pretty good."

> *JoAnne Carner, on being teamed with*
> *54-year-old Jim Albus and being tied*
> *for lead in a mixed-doubles event*

"At my age, I've got to get these while I can."
> *Dale Eggeling, on winning a tournament at age 43*

"A lot of players aren't going to be lying about their ages anymore."
> *Vicki Fergon, on leading the du Maurier classic at age 41. (Several others over 40 were high up on the leader board.)*

"The girl I beat was three."
> *Vicki Goetz-Ackerman, on not being impressed with herself for winning her first tournament at age five*

"They're all the same. They're tall, big, have long legs and a big arc, and they hit the ball a thousand miles."
> *Shelley Hamlin, longtime LPGA pro, on young players*

"It's a little scary watching the rookies today. I'm glad I'm closer to the end of my career than the beginning."
> *Betsy King*

"All I know is that when I was younger I wanted to beat the old ladies out there. Now I'm the old lady."

Nancy Lopez, at age 41

"The only thing I like about that number is that it's a good score to turn in for nine holes."

Liselotte Neumann, on turning 30

"Of course, I can say individually, I hate them."

Alice Ritzman, nonwinner on the LPGA pro tour, on the young stars of the game

"I predated college golf."

Anne Sanders, amateur champion, at age 52

"I'm not going to use the word *senior*, because our age group is 40 and over. Call it prime of life."

Hollis Stacy, on a senior LPGA tour

"It's pretty neat to see the kids doing well. Except I hate it when they call me Grandma."

Jan Stephenson, at age 47, on the young Australian players on the tour

"Now I'm just a player who's married with three kids. They can't just hand me a deal with Toys 'R' Us or a diaper maker."

Laura Baugh, on not having the glamorous endorsements she had early in her career

"I haven't been offered any spots [ads], but I can guarantee you I wouldn't turn any of them down."
Jeff Cable, Se Ri Pak's caddie

"They'll take a guy on the minitour over a woman."

Debbi Koyama, LPGA pro, on endorsement deals

"Last year I found myself scheduling tournaments around commercials rather than commercials around tournaments."

Nancy Lopez, after the success of her rookie year

"Hit it as hard as you can and we'll straighten it out later."

> *Jill Briles-Hinton, long hitter on tour, on receiving the best advice of her career when she was eight years old*

"If you swing badly but score well and win, don't change a thing."

> *Nancy Lopez, repeating advice she received from Lee Trevino*

"If I can advise Karrie on anything, I'd [tell her to] get on some antibiotics right now."

> *Dottie Pepper, advising Karrie Webb after Webb jumped into the water, after winning the Dinah Shore Tournament. Pepper had an ear infection for a month after winning the year before.*

"I try to make great golf shots. I couldn't leave a putt short if you tied me."

Amy Alcott

"I hate laying up. I hate leaving putts short. . . . I'm just an all-out attack."

Laura Davies

"Grip it and rip it."

Laura Davies, describing her strategy

"It's good to see good golf. I want to beat people at their best, not at their worst. Well, actually, I just want to beat people."

Tammie Green

"Amy Alcott is about as aggressive as a used car salesman."

Thomas Bonk, columnist,
Los Angeles Times

"The best perks about this office are who you get to play golf with. I've played with Jack Nicklaus, Arnold Palmer, Raymond Floyd, Amy Alcott."

President Bill Clinton

"Players would stop on the practice range to watch Alcott hit iron shots."

Steve Hershey, columnist, USA Today

"If she were a two-year-old racehorse, I'd rank her now."

*Walter Keller, Amy's trainer, when
she turned pro at age 18*

"No one from anywhere played the game with the pure joy of Amy Alcott."

Jim Murray, columnist,
Los Angeles Times

"Amy has pressure on her constantly, like a howitzer on her head."

> *Hollis Stacy, on the pressure,*
> *before the eligibility requirements*
> *were changed, on Alcott to win a*
> *tournament to get into the Hall*
> *of Fame*

HELEN ALFREDSSON

"She's got everything: height, strength, and a great putting stroke. And she has that rare Nordic fire."

> *Amy Alcott, on Alfredsson*

"An Italian race car driver in rush-hour traffic."

> *Anonymous, on the excitable nature*
> *of Alfredsson*

"A lot of people think about doing things. Helen does them. She seems to enjoy speeding through life."

> *Liselotte Neumann*

ALLERGIES

"The one that wasn't moving."

> *Amy Alcott, asked which ball she hit*
> *after complaining that she was seeing*
> *two balls because of her pollen*
> *allergies*

DONNA ANDREWS

"If she was a little more consistent, she'd be a metronome."

> *Gary D'Amato, Milwaukee Journal*
> *columnist, on Andrews's consistency*

"I need to find out what Donna had for dinner on Wednesday night."

> *Cindy Figg-Currier, on Donna*
> *Andrews's first-round 64 in a*
> *tournament*

AUTOGRAPHS

"Usually they have to ask if I'm a golfer."

> *Jamie Mullet, LPGA pro, after being*
> *besieged by autograph requests after*
> *a good performance in a tournament*

"I get them to autograph my hat. They really like to do that."

> *Lisa Walters, LPGA pro, on asking*
> *kids to sign her hat after she grants*
> *their autograph requests*

"Just make sure you let them know I'm not endorsing it."

> *Karrie Webb, after putting her*
> *autograph on a book titled*
> How to Cheat in Golf

AWARDS

"I thought you had to be dead to win that."

> *JoAnne Carner, on winning the Bob*
> *Jones Award for sportsmanship*

"I'll have my name on the trophy whether I win or lose."

> *Laura Davies, on the best thing about a tournament being named after her*

"To my various playing partners and opponents, this award in no way improves my lack of skill in sports, so all bets are off."

> *Jamie Farr, on receiving an LPGA award for promoting women's golf*

"I'm hoping that I'm presenting it to me."

> *Nancy Lopez, on being designated as future host of the Chick-fil-A Tour event*

"It tasted a little chemical at first."

> *Patty Sheehan, on drinking from the LPGA trophy after winning the 1993 championship*

"I think I'm living in a dream and I hope I never wake up."

> *Annika Sorenstam, on winning the Player of the Year Award for the second year in a row*

BACKACHE

"This keeps the disc from going disco."
> *Muffin Spencer-Devlin, on crouching*
> *while talking to the media because of*
> *a bad back*

BAD HOLES

"I would have liked to dive into the water with my bag and sink as quickly as possible."
> *Robin Burke, amateur, on taking a*
> *10 at the U.S. Open*

"I left it in, I left it in, and I left it in, and then I got it out."
> *Laura Davies, asked how it took her*
> *three shots to get out of a bunker*

"It was nice to be in the shade a little bit."
> *Tammie Green, on hitting a tree*
> *during a hot day in a tournament*

"It was like *Nightmare on Elm Street, Part Seven.*"
Caroline Keggi, on shooting a
triple-bogey seven

"I got myself into some grass that was taller than
I was."
Alison Nicholas, on being five feet
tall and bogeying a hole because
of the grass

"I was looking for my ball in the rough, but I was
hoping that the ground would swell up and suck
me in."
Karen Stupples, on losing a
tournament because of two miserable
shots in a row

BAD ROUNDS

"I was playing hockey there for a while."
Sally Dee, after a bogey and double
bogey on consecutive holes

"When I hit iron, I say goodbye to ball."
Ayako Okamoto

"My tee shots made me work a lot. My putting was a problem, too. Otherwise, everything is OK."
Se Ri Pak, after a bad round

"I was a good spectator today."
Kelly Robbins, on a bad round

"You don't know what you can do to stop the bleeding. Thank God, you know you run out of holes and you can go home and sleep."
Patty Sheehan, after a bad round

"On a bad round when you walk off the 18th green, you should walk out the door and close it and walk into a new room."
Wendy Ward

"The good news when you don't play well in a 54-hole tournament is that you get a morning tee time on the second day. The bad news is that you're there because you didn't play well."
Karen Weiss

"It was sort of unenthusiastic, unless you like to see someone leaving herself a lot of 40-foot putts."

Karen Weiss, on a round of
uninspired play

BASEBALL

"That's over the Green Wall. The Red Sox need a few of them."

Pat Bradley, after hitting a ball over
a fence during a practice round

"My batting swing is too much like my golf swing."

Akiko Fukushima, on loving baseball
but not being a great hitter

"She is great with kids. I think when you're great with kids, you can't be too bad."

Nancy Lopez, on Marge Schott,
the controversial former
Cincinnati Reds owner

"We were in some lady's driveway."

> *Dawn Coe-Jones, on being allergic to bees and running away from a swarm of them on one of the holes she was playing*

"I said, 'Oh no, I'm going to die on the 18th green.'"

> *Hollis Stacy, describing her reaction to a swarm of bees on the 18th hole of a tournament*

PATTY BERG

"I wouldn't change anything. I couldn't be this lucky twice."

> *Patty Berg, on her great career*

"Babe Zaharias couldn't carry her clubs."

> *Mickey Wright, on the golf game of Patty Berg*

"This course is so tight, it squeaks."
*Connie Chillemi, on the narrow
fairways at the course*

BEVERAGE OF CHOICE

"Well, there must be a bottle of Scotch over there
in the bushes."
*Babe Didrikson, on slicing a shot to
the right*

"Promoting beer comes easy. Promoting the LPGA
tour comes even easier."
*Lorie Kane, on being a former sales
agent for a brewery*

"I go to the different wineries [in Napa Valley]. As
for collecting, I end up drinking most of it."
*Liselotte Neumann, on wine
collecting, a special interest of hers*

"I have no expertise other than I enjoy good wine and I have very expensive tastes."

> Alice Ritzman, on her dream of being a winemaker

"I sneaked her a beer from the bar."

> Lee Trevino, asked if he ever helped Nancy Lopez. This happened when she was 18 and not allowed in the clubhouse.

BIRDIES

"If you make birdies, you'll stay up there. If you don't, a lot of people are going to pass you."

> Becky Iverson

"It makes your dinner taste better."

> Nancy Lopez, on getting a birdie on the 18th hole

"Nineteen fifty-seven—the year I was born."

> *Nancy Lopez, asked, after a 1985*
> *tournament, the last time she did not*
> *have at least one birdie in a round*
> *of golf*

"My fiancé showed up at number 12. He'll be out here tomorrow for the whole round."

> *Barb Thomas, on getting birdies on*
> *the 12th, 14th, 15th, and 18th holes*

BLACKWOLF RUN

"Every hole has a different personality. You just have to grit your teeth and rip it. There are too many things to intimidate you."

> *Nancy Lopez, on Blackwolf Run Golf*
> *Course in Milwaukee*

"The rough at Blackwolf Run appears to be more golden retriever than rottweiler."

> *Bob Wolfley, columnist,*
> Milwaukee Journal

JANE BLALOCK

"I can feel Jane going for my throat right now."
> *Carolyn Hill, on holding a one-shot*
> *lead over Blalock going into the final*
> *round of a tournament*

BOGEY MAN

"It's hard to have a lot of confidence out there
when you're standing on the tee of a hole that the
day before you made quadruple bogey on."
> *Jennifer Hanna, LPGA pro*

"I've taken bigger falls in bigger tournaments
than this."
> *Rosie Jones, on a quadruple bogey*

"I had a brain cramp. I felt pretty stupid."
> *Lenore Muraoka, one of only two*
> *people to bogey the 12th hole of the*
> *U.S. Open*

BOWLING

"It was like a 270 game."
> *Barb Mucha, an avid bowler, on*
> *shooting a 66*

PAT BRADLEY

"It's a rare honor to have a tournament named for you—usually it's reserved for the very rich or very dead."
> *Tony Kornheiser, on the Pat Bradley*
> *Invitational Tournament*

"She can't win everything. But she is not the ideal person to be chasing."
> *Deb Richard, on trailing Pat Bradley*
> *going into the final day of a*
> *tournament*

"Pat Bradley may be the toughest athlete."
> *Dr. Bob Rotella, on the inner strength*
> *of pro athletes he's worked with*

"Death, taxes, and Pat Bradley's name on the leader board."

Val Skinner, on the inevitabilities of life

BRAIN DRAIN

"Because I was stupid then."

Laura Davies, asked why she used to use her driver for every hole

BRITISH OPEN

"I'd cash in most of my 56 victories for this one."

Laura Davies, asked what the British Open means to her

BUSINESS

"Today even women have to have a responsible golf game—it's part of the corporate inventory."
Nancy Oliver, founder of the
Executive Women's Golf Association

"If you don't play golf, you'll end up in charge of lunch."
Jan Thompson, head of Wilson's golf
division, on the importance of women
in the golf business

BY THE TIME I GET TO PHOENIX

"I think I'm going to retire here."
Laura Davies, after winning the
LPGA Standard Register PING in
Phoenix for a fourth straight year

25

"I don't know why that putt hung on to the edge. I'm a clean liver. It must be my caddie."

JoAnne Carner

"What's not to like? There's action—you get to be outside, travel, see some great golf and some not so great golf."

Andrea Doddato, Rosie Jones's caddie

"It got confusing. I really wasn't sure when I was supposed to be the caddie and when I was supposed to be the husband."

John Dormann, former caddie for
Dana Loflend-Dormann, his wife

"I couldn't figure it out. I wore deodorant and everything."

Marlene Hagge, on having five
caddies in one day at a tournament

"Who would you rather look at all day—Cindy Flom or Craig Stadler?"

Tom Hansen, on why he enjoys being
a caddie for women

"He caddied for me briefly when we first dated. It wasn't pretty."

> Denise Killeen, on her husband,
> John, who is Meg Mallon's caddie

"If it weren't for the money, I'd retire and go caddie for my wife."

> Ray Knight, former major league
> baseball player and husband of
> Nancy Lopez

"He still caddies for me. He carries the bag from the trunk of the car to the golf course."

> Nancy Lopez, after firing her
> husband, Ray Knight, as her caddie

"I don't make many mistakes when he's watching. When he's caddying, it's different."

> Nancy Lopez, on why she fired her
> husband as her caddie

"Once we get to the course, we're not brother and sister. We're caddie and player."

> J. C. McGann, caddie for his sister,
> Michelle

"It's too much of a crutch for me and too easy for me to yell at him."

> *Dottie Pepper, on having her*
> *husband as her caddie*

"We basically sucked today."

> *Karrie Webb, on her and caddie Evan*
> *Minster having a bad day with shot*
> *selection*

"We had guys quitting and going with other agencies, the FBI, state and county police. My other agency turned out to be the LPGA."

> *Rich White, former police officer who*
> *was a caddie for Jan Stephenson*

"A lot of these players could win with a wheelbarrow carrying their clubs."

> *Eddie Williams, caddie for*
> *Hollis Stacy*

"I read now and again that I'm the new Big Mama. Obviously, it's a compliment to be compared to JoAnne . . . but there can only be one."
Laura Davies

"When JoAnne joined the LPGA tour, they were playing with hickory shafts."
Tammie Green, poking fun at the age of her friend JoAnne Carner

"JoAnne is such a brilliant shotmaker and fighter that whenever she loses, put a bet down on her the next time."
Nancy Lopez

"JoAnne Carner has never had a boring round of golf. Every one [tournament] has had the adventure of a lion-country safari."
Jim Murray

CHILD'S PLAY

"I thought the world of golf was one of Hermans and Byrons. The name Amy didn't fit in."

>*Amy Alcott, on watching golf as a child*

"Where's mine?"

>*Patty Berg, at age 12, after her younger brother received a set of golf clubs*

"If it wasn't fun, we wouldn't stay out here. It's like going to the park as a kid."

>*Marianne Morris, LPGA pro, asked by a child if she enjoyed golf*

CIRCUS ACT

"Once in a while I'd miss, but that made it more exciting."

>*Diane Patterson, LPGA pro who was formerly part of a trapeze act*

"I decided it was easier to swing on the ground than in the air."

> *Diane Patterson, on why she gave up the trapeze to play golf*

"I'd probably be a fat lady in the circus if it weren't for golf."

> *Kathy Whitworth, on her huge appetite as a child until she started playing golf*

CLOTHES HORSE

"It clashes with everything I have."

> *Danielle Ammaccapane, upon being awarded a green jacket for winning a tournament*

"We're like actresses. Since we're always in the public eye, we can't afford to be seen in dated clothes."

> *Donna Caponi, when asked why she and her sister Janet always bought golf clothes early in their careers*

"I'm still pretty young, and I'm OK compared to the older players. Later on, it bothered me a little."

Mi Hyun Kim, when asked why she wore shorts and short sleeves in a tournament in cold conditions

"We should all try to look more ladylike on the course. Being thought of as anything but a woman definitely frosts me."

Carol Mann, on dressing well

"In America, nobody cares if my shirt is gross or my pants are broken."

Ayako Okamoto, on the privacy she has in the United States as compared to her homeland of Japan

"All I know is that I look at those clips and see what I am wearing, and I go, 'Oh God, Oh God.'"

Hollis Stacy, on the many changes in golf fashions over the years

"We made a deal that I wouldn't tell him how to design clothes and he wouldn't tell me how to play golf."

> *Tina Toms, LPGA pro, on wearing the clothes of her husband, designer Joey Rodolfo*

"The only tough thing is that it takes me 45 minutes to put an outfit together. I've got to get the argyles, the sweater, and the shirts to go together."

> *Jo Ann Washam, on wearing knickers*

CLUBHOUSE

"I wish I could say I was outraged about it, but I'm not. I'm trying to get health care for the children of the country, not worrying about Burning Tree."

> *Donna Shalala, Clinton cabinet secretary, expressing her feelings on Burning Tree Country Club in Washington not allowing women as members*

"I'd rather struggle on my own. I'd hate to have someone help me destroy my game."

> *Laura Davies, asked if she*
> *considered getting an instructor*
> *for her short game*

"If you take a man and a woman with the same talent, I can get the lady to hit the ball quicker than the man. Because he's looking for detail all the time. She isn't."

> *Manuel de la Torre, legendary*
> *golf coach*

"Judy has a notebook . . . of lessons from me. She used to carry it around with her. Now she carries me around."

> *Gardner Dickinson, who became*
> *Judy Clark's coach and then her*
> *husband*

"I refuse to be a tennis ball. If she doesn't want to work with me, fine, but make up your damned mind."

> *David Leadbetter, on being fired as coach by Se Ri Pak and then being reconsidered as her coach*

COMMISSIONER

"Only my backswing."

> *Charles Mechem, LPGA commissioner, when asked if there was anything embarrassing in his past*

COMPETITION

"There's nothing I can do about the other players unless I put a firecracker in someone's bag on their golf swing."

> *Amy Alcott, on competition*

"I liked to arm-wrestle the boys, and I always beat them."

> *Helen Alfredsson, on being*
> *competitive even as a child*

"Competition is even more fun than golf. I like going down to the wire knowing somebody's going to choke, and hoping it's not me."

> *JoAnne Carner*

"The only thing I never learned from Billy Martin was how to knock a guy out in a bar."

> *JoAnne Carner, on how her friend*
> *Billy Martin helped teach her how*
> *to compete against other players*

"You learn to read your opponents. I know that with certain players if I hit the tee shot on the first hole as hard as I could, I'd win the match."

> *JoAnne Carner*

"I am out to beat everybody in sight, and that is just what I'm going to do."

> *Babe Didrikson, before a tournament*

"You cannot sleep one minute out here."
Rosie Jones, on the competition
getting better all the time

"It doesn't matter if I'm playing for first or tenth—
wherever I'm at, I want to beat whoever is in front
of me."
Rosie Jones

"Even though you're sort of competing against
each other, it all comes down to how you play
the course."
Michele Redman

"I played the way my dad taught me. . . . When you
get somebody down, you step on 'em."
Louise Suggs

"When you get somebody down, step on their
throat or they'll get up and whip your fanny."
Louise Suggs

CONCENTRATION

"I couldn't concentrate. It was too pretty."

> *Muffin Spencer-Devlin, on losing a big lead on a beautiful day*

"I struggled a couple of times with my concentration."

> *Karrie Webb, on how her family's presence affected her concentration in a tournament. She shot a 31 in the first nine.*

CONFIDENCE

"I build confidence when I practice a variety of shots—hitting it high or low, working the ball. My confidence is built on knowing I can effectively work the ball in any circumstances."

> *JoAnne Carner*

"Even in my good tournaments, I'm not comfortable with a six-shot lead with five holes to play."

Laura Davies

CONGENIALITY

"Smiling face, nice to people, helping people. They remember me, my face."

Se Ri Pak, on what she wants her impact to be as a golfer

"When you're growing up, your coach doesn't say, 'Oh, after you make this putt, you have to practice smiling, so when you're out playing professional golf, you'll be able to do it.'"

Karrie Webb, on being criticized for not smiling enough

COOK

"I didn't get these calluses to spend my life baking cakes."

*Amy Alcott, on deciding that
her career goal was not to be
a homemaker*

"I rate myself as a super cook . . . if the can is easy to open and the label is easy to read."

*Dede Owens, LPGA player, asked if
she was a good cook*

COUNTRY CLUB
OF INDIANAPOLIS

"The course is like shooting down a bowling alley. I kept seeing monsters in the rough."

*Hollis Stacy, on the Country Club of
Indianapolis, home of the 1978 U.S.
Women's Open*

"You get a certain golf course sometimes, and it's like you can write your name on it."

> *Dale Eggeling, on doing well on*
> *certain courses*

"He can be a severe, sadistic golf course architect."

> *Cindy Figg-Currier, on Pete Dye*

"You think when you're making birdies you're moving up, but today you feel like you're just spinning your wheels."

> *Denise Killeen, after a round in*
> *which everyone scored well*

"When I can remember every hole."

> *Nancy Lopez, offering her definition*
> *of a good golf course*

"The son of Pete Dye is my partner, so I should have a big in because I know exactly how his father's strategy works."

> *Jan Stephenson, on playing on a Pete*
> *Dye course. Dye's son is her partner*
> *in designing courses.*

"We are not trying to destroy players. We are trying to identify the best ones."

> *Sandy Tatum, former USGA*
> *president, on some of the tough*
> *courses played by LPGA members*

"The way the LPGA is treated, if we play on a course and shoot 20-under, then the course is too easy, not that we played great golf."

> *Karrie Webb*

CURSES

"I don't think so. Some things are better left unsaid."

> *Helen Alfredsson, after reporters*
> *asked for a translation when she*
> *hit a bad shot and started cursing*
> *in Swedish*

"I was trying to add a little color. Unfortunately, what I added was off-color."

> *Lori Garbacz, LPGA pro, after she*
> *shouted obscenities while on ESPN*

"She occasionally asks the ball something in Swedish that I don't believe I could write even if I could translate it."

Jim Murray, on the cursing of
Helen Alfredsson

CUT

═══════════════════════════════

"The wheels came off for Big Mama."

JoAnne Carner, on missing a rare cut
in an event

"Normally I would have been distraught . . . but when I realized I wouldn't be playing on the weekend, I was delighted."

Judy Dickinson, on missing a cut
after her twins were born

"I don't know what to do on weekends."

Annika Sorenstam, after a rare
missed cut

BETH DANIEL

"I have always looked up to Beth, both as a player and physically—she is a lot taller than I am."
Patty Sheehan

DATING GAME

"Just tall ones."
Michelle McGann, when asked if she went out only with athletes after dating a 6'10" basketball player and 6'6" football player

"It's like swinging at a golf ball and quitting on the shot . . . like there's no follow-through."
Sharon Moran, on dating when you're in town for a tournament

LAURA DAVIES

"I can only dream of hitting it as far as she does."
Donna Andrews

"When she hit the ball, the earth shook."
JoAnne Carner, on the first time she saw Davies hit a ball

"If she ever says she can't putt again, I'm coming after her."
John Daly, after Davies hit a clutch putt that helped them win a mixed-doubles competition

"She would keep her card and probably win a couple of tournaments."
John Daly, on how Davies would do on the men's tour

"She is the player who can take it deep, the force, the franchise."
Larry Dorman

"You're the woman."

Nancy Lopez, after Davies hit a very long drive

"I'm a pretty long driver compared to the other girls, but I'm not close to Laura."

Nancy Lopez

"If she used a driver off the tee and kept it in the fairway, the rest of us would be playing for second most of the time."

Nancy Lopez

"She doesn't yell 'fore,' she yells 'lift off.'"

Jim Murray, on Davies's lengthy drives

"She can do everything Nick Faldo can do and make sure the sun never sets on the British golf empire."

Jim Murray, on Davies

"Watching Laura Davies hit a golf ball is like watching Dempsey throw a punch."

Jim Murray

"Laura's golf is on another planet."
Ayako Okamoto

"I think they should rename the place for her.
I played as well as I could play. She played
one better."
*Julie Piers, on Davies winning the
LPGA Championship*

"Most of us always think we hit it further than we
actually do. But it seems that Laura Davies hits it
as far as she and everybody else thinks she does."
Judy Rankin

"Like David and Goliath."
*Patty Sheehan, on the
difference between her drives
and Laura Davies's*

"Who would have thought that two little peewees
could beat the big Laura."
*Patty Sheehan, after she and
Rosie Jones won the Solheim Cup
Match against Laura Davies and
a teammate*

"She couldn't beat these men. She couldn't even beat the women now."

> *Lee Trevino, on Davies playing a*
> *tournament on the men's tour*

BABE DIDRIKSON

"Our sport grew because of Babe, because she had so much flair and color. With Babe there was never a dull minute."

> *Patty Berg*

"She possessed that type of charisma that Arnold Palmer has when he walks up a fairway."

> *Patty Berg, on Babe*

"Babe, on any given day, could beat any of them by sheer force of will. She could be as good as she had to be."

> *Fred Corcoran, longtime promoter*

"Implausible is the adjective which best befits the Babe."

> *Arthur Daly, columnist,*
> New York Times

"I just take off my girdle and beat the ball, sir."

Babe Didrikson, when asked how she
could hit a ball 300 yards

"Yeah, dolls."

Babe Didrikson, when asked if
there was something she didn't play

"I hit the ball like a girl, and she hits it like a man."

Bob Hope, on Didrikson

"There is only one Babe Didrikson, and there has never been another in her class—or [who] can come close to her class."

Grantland Rice, legendary
sports columnist

"The Babe is without any question the athletic phenomenon of all time, man or woman."

Grantland Rice

"I knew of only one golfer who practiced more than Babe, and that was Ben Hogan."

Gene Sarazen

"She was too much show business to ever develop a really sweet swing. She wanted to wallop the ball, because that played to the public."

Gene Sarazen

"We don't have a real character in the group—somebody like the Babe to kid the gallery and bring in the fans."

Marilynn Smith, on the problems of the pro tour in the '60s

"She was so cocky, everyone else was in awe of her."

Louise Suggs, on not being intimidated by the Babe

DOCTOR, DOCTOR

"I hate doctors, especially ones who are going to be digging my eyes out."

Laura Davies, on why she waited so long to have eye surgery

"I'm sure they're happy I didn't play. I still have a fever."

> *Meg Mallon, on getting sick the day before she was supposed to play a pro-am event with several doctors*

DOG EAT DOG

"My dogs . . . don't care what you shoot. I shoot a 66 and everyone will love me. But if I shoot an 86, probably only the dogs love me."

> *Jill Briles-Hinton, on her first-round 66 in the U.S. Open*

DRIVES

"I found out fast that they don't pay you for how far you hit it."

> *Caroline Blaylock, on being a long hitter in her rookie year*

"We hit a few, and they stop talking."

Laura Davies, on pro-am partners
who challenge her to drive

"Luckily, it was downwind and with a lie.
Otherwise, I'd be off being drug-tested."

Laura Davies, after driving a
4-iron 240 yards

"When I hit my driver, I hear it pretty much every
hole. I never get tired of it."

Laura Davies, on enthusiasm from
the gallery when she drives the ball

"It was downhill, downwind, and downgrain."

Laura Davies, on hitting a ball over
350 yards

"It's not that I'm better than the women. I'm longer
than them."

Laura Davies

"I ended up in plenty of swimming pools and
dog dishes."

Laura Davies, on her drives in the
early years

"Maybe if there's a hurricane behind me."
> *Vicki Goetze-Ackerman, asked if she could reach the green of a 419-yard hole in two shots*

"I guess as long as they keep comparing me just to his driving, it's all right."
> *Michelle McGann, on comparisons between her and John Daly*

DU MAURIER CLASSIC

"Rodney Dangerfield should be the poster boy for the LPGA's du Maurier Classic."
> *Amy Nutt, Sports Illustrated reporter, on the lack of respect for this tournament, which is one of the majors*

EAGLE HAS LANDED

"I stood there and watched as it went right into the hole. I mean, it was ridiculous."

Carol Semple Thompson,
amateur golfer, on making an
eagle 2 on a hole

EARLY ROUNDS

"I'm a firm believer that a tournament doesn't start until the weekend—especially that last nine on Sunday."

Beth Daniel, on not feeling excited
about a first-round lead

"This is only the first quarter. We play four quarters."

Michelle McGann, on leading a
tournament after the first round

"I'm usually the rabbit in the greyhound race. I start off real fast. I'm usually an unknown on Sunday."

> *Lenore Rittenhouse, on losing a playoff final*

EARLY YEARS

"When I first played, there were five of us playing for a total purse of $500. The rest were amateurs."
> *Patty Berg*

"It wasn't at all difficult to be accepted as a woman golfer, because there just weren't that many women playing."

> *Glenna Collot Vare, on golf in the 1920s*

"We need to change women's to ladies'—it's more appropriate."

> *Fred Corcoran, president of the Women's Professional Golf Association, started in 1949*

"About everybody, most likely."

> *Babe Didrikson, when asked what*
> *sponsors she would play with during*
> *an event*

"We were just a bunch of stubborn women who loved golf and figured we could make it happen."

> *Marlene Hagge, one of the pioneers*
> *of the women's pro tour*

"I can remember when the lady's purse was a purse."

> *Bob Hope*

"We were like a band of gypsies."

> *Betty Jameson, one of the pioneers*
> *of the women's pro tour*

"If you put the hole in a divot, you had to make sure a cow didn't find it first."

> *Jim Murray, on the early years of*
> *the LPGA*

"People didn't turn pro back then unless they were good players, because the only appeal was golf."

> *Betsy Rawls*

"We fought like cats all the time."

Louise Suggs, on the LPGA founders

"They get mad if they don't have the right food in the locker room. . . . We were lucky if we got peanut butter and crackers."

Louise Suggs, on today's players

"I wouldn't trade my experiences for anything, but I don't know that I'd want to go through them again."

Louise Suggs

"I would equate it to trying to dunk a basketball from the standing position. And they reached pretty high."

Ty Votaw, LPGA commissioner, on women's golf in the early years

"I had a little Sunday bag, and I didn't even have a complete set of clubs."

Kathy Whitworth, on her first LPGA tournament in 1958

"I'm thrilled about the way things are now. Hey, I remember when the LPGA had to play Fresno."
Kathy Whitworth

EGO

"When I first turned pro, they called me cocky, but mostly I was good."
Amy Alcott

"You don't think for one minute I'm gonna miss that, do you?"

Babe Didrikson, on having to hit a 30-foot putt to win a tournament (she did)

"Amy, how are you going to get an 11 on this hole?"

> *Hollis Stacy, to Amy Alcott, who*
> *was leading Stacy by 10 strokes*
> *going into the last hole of*
> *a tournament*

EMOTIONS

"For so long, every shot had been an adventure."

> *Helen Alfredsson, on trying to play*
> *with less emotion*

"I like to live the game."

> *Helen Alfredsson, on having problems*
> *not showing emotion*

"I try to temper it a little bit when there's a rules official around."

> *Juli Inkster, on being an*
> *emotional player*

"I don't mind the adrenaline. I'm happy waking up."

Annika Sorenstam, on not needing to be a thrill seeker to get her kicks

EVEN PAR

"Nothing wonderful happened and nothing terrible happened. Even par never hurts you."

Dottie Pepper, on shooting an even par in the second round of a tournament

EVERYBODY'S WORKING FOR THE WEEKEND

"The weekend is always going to be the weekend. The competition gets tougher and tougher and the field seems to separate."

Helen Alfredsson

EXERCISE

"I polish the boat."

> *JoAnne Carner, on polishing her*
> *42-foot boat as her exercise routine*

EXPECTATIONS

"A top player plays good and—whooom—people
think they always play very high."

> *Se Ri Pak*

EYE FOR AN EYE

"Friends would wave at me from across the
green and I wasn't waving back. They thought
I was rude."

> *Laura Davies, on her poor eyesight*
> *before she underwent laser surgery to*
> *correct it*

"I used to just hit the ball and ask the caddie, 'Where did that one go?'"

> *Laura Davies, on her bad eyesight*

FAMILY

"She's the one who's smiling after shooting a 78. When you've got kids to worry about, a double bogey isn't the end of the world."

> *Myra Blackwelder, on spotting a touring pro with kids*

"They are not very competitive. They mostly hit and giggle, hit and giggle."

> *Jill Briles-Hinton, LPGA pro, on how her two sisters play golf*

"If I want any sympathy, I have to call up my parents."

> *Beth Daniel, after winning a tournament despite a bad shoulder*

"It's a lot easier to think about birdies when you don't have to think about diapers."

Juli Inkster, on juggling being a mother and a pro golfer

"I don't need fanfare. I just want to play golf. And I want to be Mom."

Juli Inkster, asked about the lack of fanfare for her accomplishments

"I only work half a year and I get the other half off. I have got it pretty easy as far as being the working woman and making it."

Juli Inkster

"Ayako Okamoto. But you're second, Mom."

Ashley Knight, daughter of Nancy Lopez, asked at age five who her favorite golfer was

"They love softball, so that causes some pretty ugly golf swings."

Nancy Lopez, asked if her daughters will play on the pro tour

"My place was to sit and listen to everybody. I'm not used to the attention being on myself."

> *Meg Mallon, on being the sixth of six children*

"I wouldn't mind being related, though, especially to his money."

> *Sandra Palmer, who is constantly asked if she is related to Arnold*

"For a long while, my son thought only women played golf."

> *Judy Rankin, whose son traveled with her on the pro tour as a youngster*

"She never asks what I shot."

> *Patty Sheehan, on one of the great joys of adopting a baby girl*

"I think he wants a Sorenstam to win."

> *Charlotta Sorenstam, on her father, who had flown from Sweden to watch a tournament in which she was tied with her sister Annika for the lead*

"At least it was easy for him—he only had to watch two groups."

Charlotta Sorenstam, on her dad

"I grew up in chaos, in a large family, and I think that has been a distinct advantage, because every day is different, every hole is different, every feeling is different."

Hollis Stacy

"We never stay together at a tournament anymore. That would cramp my style."

Tillie Stacy, Hollis's mom

"They've been practicing more than I have."

Karrie Webb, on her parents and friends being amateur partners in a tournament

FAN CLUB

"I like many people. They watch me and then big loud."

Se Ri Pak

"That's the last time I've ever given anybody a pep talk before a final round."

> *Amy Alcott, on having given her opponent, Sherri Turner, a pep talk before the final round and then losing to her*

"I've never had an easy 18 holes in the final round."

> *Amy Alcott, asked if she had an easy final round after winning the Dinah Shore*

"I want to win like a champion, or otherwise I don't want to win."

> *Amy Alcott, asked if she would play it safe with a big lead going into the final round of a tournament*

FIRST ROUND

"The first round is like a novel. We're in Chapter One, and the characters are being identified. Tomorrow, the plot thickens."
Amy Alcott

"I might be the leading money winner after the first round this year, which doesn't make you a dime."
Meg Mallon, on her fast starts

FISHING

"I feel great. I made enough money to go fishing."
JoAnne Carner, on finishing second in the Dinah Shore, two days before turning 50

"I got so depressed. They have some huge bass in there."
Kelly Robbins, when asked what she thought of the lake on the 18th hole of the Dinah Shore

FLAWS

"If you've got any flaws and you're playing on the tour, they will come up very quickly and knock you all the way down."
Patty Berg

FOOD

"My pants are a little snugger this week."
Dale Eggeling, on her fondness for the food on a tour stop in Tucson

"Important for me after golf is eating, and so I have to find a good restaurant."
Se Ri Pak, on her priorities after a tournament

"It's the Mexican food. It's lousy on the East Coast."
Dottie Pepper, responding jokingly after being asked why she seems to play so well in the Welch's/Circle K Tournament in Arizona

"I like the ice cream."

Val Skinner, explaining why she
enjoys playing the Friendly's
Tournament in Massachusetts

FOOTBALL

"I'm very glad I gave up football, or I wouldn't be here tonight."

Patty Berg, who excelled in football
when she was growing up

FRIENDSHIP

"When you spend four or five hours on a golf course with somebody, you run the whole gamut of emotions together. . . . By the end of the round, you have a buddy."

Jane Blalock

FUTURES TOUR

"Like a major leaguer going back to A ball. Not Triple A—single A."

Kim Williams, on going from the LPGA to the Futures Tour

GALLERY

"The reason they're following her is that she's always breaking something. Like par."

Furman Bisher, columnist, Atlanta Constitution, *on the huge crowds following Nancy Lopez*

"I enjoy the gallery. It keeps me relaxed. And most of the time I'm on their side of the ropes."

JoAnne Carner

"There were roars everywhere. That's wonderful if you are watching a tournament, but when you are leading a tournament—it's unsettling."

Beth Daniel

"Maybe we need to enforce a barefoot policy for the weekend."

> *Laura Davies, on noise caused by the crowd walking in desert sand during a tournament*

"People want to see you have a go. I reckon that's why they come out."

> *Laura Davies, on the big crowds she attracts*

"Now I know what the cheeseheads do in the summer. They go to golf tournaments."

> *Tammie Green, on the more than 115,000 people in attendance during the course of the U.S. Women's Open, held in Wisconsin in 1998*

"I'm not afraid of the roughs and traps, but it's so humiliating when the gallery hangs you in effigy."

> *Bob Hope, on the fans' reaction to his poor play during the LPGA pro-am*

"I might play better golf than they do, but I'm nothing without them."

> *Nancy Lopez, on the gallery*

"The roars are for Nancy. The rest of us get the meows."

> *Debbie Massey, on Nancy Lopez*

"There's a birdie noise, and then there's something better."

> *Kris Monaghan, on Martha Nause getting an eagle on the 18th hole to beat Monaghan*

"Unfortunately, I didn't hit balls outside the ropes, so I didn't get out to say hello."

> *Ayako Okamoto, on the large number of Japanese fans cheering for her*

"You think about how sweet they are and then you remember you have to hit a shot."

> *Hollis Stacy, on her adoring crowds*

"When you go in the rough as much as I do, there's people there to talk to."

> *Kris Tschetter, when asked why she is so popular with the fans*

"Some of the customers must have come disguised as trees."

> Bob Verdi, columnist for the Chicago Tribune, *on overestimates of the number of people who attended an LPGA event in Chicago*

"There were times I felt like an appendix—I was there, but I had no purpose."

> Ty Votaw, on being in a foursome with Meg Mallon, Mia Hamm, and Julie Foudy

GAMBLIN'

"Too many distractions in Las Vegas and Atlantic City."

> Amy Alcott, on coming close to, but not achieving, her 30th tour win in tournaments in Atlantic City and Las Vegas

"I usually lose money with the Red Sox every summer and then win it back in the winter with the Celtics."

> Pat Bradley

"I don't drink. I don't smoke. I don't do drugs, so I think it is all right to gamble a bit."
Laura Davies

"There's a wheel spinning somewhere."
Laura Davies, on why she was in a hurry to get off the course in a Las Vegas tournament

"Yes, you could. And you'd probably get pretty good odds on it, too."
Laura Davies, when asked if there should be a trifecta, or winning the same tournament three years in a row

"I'd like to be able to bet as much as he does."
Laura Davies, on why her idol is Michael Jordan

"If you do well, you win loads anyway."
Laura Davies, on why she never bets on herself in Great Britain, where it is legal to bet on golf

"I'm not addicted to gambling. I'm addicted to fun."

Laura Davies

"No, I hate betting on golf. I love playing for prize money, but I don't like losing my own."

Laura Davies, on betting on golf

"Thank God for that."

Laura Davies, on the 1997 U.S. Open being held in Oregon, where there are no casinos

"I don't see how. Playing this game is a gamble. Life is a gamble."

Pam Higgins, LPGA pro, when asked if her love of gambling had tarnished her golf game

"I wish they had pari-mutuel betting on this tournament. I figure I'd be about 25 to 1 and I'd lay a lot on myself."

Pam Higgins, leading after the second round of the Dinah Shore Open in 1976. She did not win the tournament.

"I'm not a heavy bettor. I bet for Coke and stuff. I choke when I play for five dollars."

Nancy Lopez

GAME FACE

"I put on my game face because that's what I need to do to win."

Betsy King, on her grim demeanor on the golf course

"When I'm out there, I don't want to show any weaknesses to my opponents—that I'm upset or struggling or whatever. From a strategy standpoint, it's important not to do that."

Betsy King

"This is not the Ice Capades. You don't fall on a double axel and get up and smile and everything's OK, you know."

Dottie Pepper, when asked about her serious expression on the golf course

GARDENING

"I am replacing all the grass I dug up when I was on the tour."

> *Marlene Hagge, on gardening in her retirement to make up for all her years of digging up grass with her shots*

GLAMOROUS LIFE

"People think it's all so glamorous. But they don't see us at the laundromat."

> *Kate Golden, LPGA pro, on life on the tour*

VICKI GOETZE-ACKERMAN

"A swing so flawless, it quickens the heart."

> *Michael Madden, columnist, Boston Globe, on the swing of Vicki Goetze-Ackerman*

GOLF CARTS

"I figured if I started golfing I'd get to drive the cart more often."

Pat Hurst, on her stepdad letting her drive his golf cart at age 11

GOLF EQUIPMENT

"When that baby goes and I have to put it to sleep, it'll be a sad day."

Amy Alcott, on her 7-wood

"It's sort of a third arm. I've even thought of insuring it with Lloyd's of London."

Amy Alcott, on that same 7-wood

"I buy maybe two pairs of shoes a year, and my golf shoes have holes in them."

Amy Alcott

"I don't think there's any technology better than believing in yourself."

> *Amy Alcott, on playing with the same clubs for years*

"They're like a set of old friends. They don't get old, they just get more character."

> *Amy Alcott, on her golf clubs*

"I'm for equality on the course. There's no reason that women shouldn't suffer the same as men playing this damn game."

> *Ely Callaway, founder of a brand of women's golf equipment*

"He may have to buy another one."

> *JoAnne Carner, on using her husband's putter, which he had just bought, and taking the U.S. Open lead with it*

"I'm going to kick Don out of bed tonight, put the putter in, and if I win, Don can sleep with me tomorrow night."

> *JoAnne Carner, on her husband and having the lead going into the final round of the Dinah Shore*

"Desi."

Rosie Jones, asked the name of her
new putter after she replaced the first
one, which was named Lucy

"You've got to be an engineer anymore to
understand the equipment."

Hollis Stacy, on the new equipment
in golf

"They are not shotmakers like we were. They just
stand up, hit the ball, and go chase it."

Louise Suggs, on today's players and
the better golf equipment they use

GOLF WISDOM

"Golf became my trustiest companion, my best
friend."

Amy Alcott, on what golf meant to
her when she was growing up

"In golf you either play real good or not good. It's a black-and-white sport. It doesn't have much gray area."

Amy Alcott

"I love golf. You have to, because you have to play it with passion. But you can't have passion without love."

Amy Alcott

"There's no feeling in the world like smacking that ball out there exactly where you want."

Amy Alcott

"As long as you try to give 100 percent and make your decisions, one day it's going to give you 63 and one day it's going to give you 76."

Helen Alfredsson

"A lot of great players don't win Super Bowls."

Amy Benz, on playing more than 300 matches and not winning a tournament

"There isn't anything I don't like about golf."

Patty Berg

"It's not how fast you get there, but how long you stay."

> *Patty Berg on being at the top*
> *of her game*

"You're always learning new ideas, new methods. It keeps you young."

> *Patty Berg*

"Golf's a character builder. Golf's all you, nobody else."

> *JoAnne Carner*

"Never hurry when it counts."

> *JoAnne Carner*

"It's the ability to forget about a bad swing and think about good stuff."

> *Laura Davies, on why great players*
> *win more than others*

"The best part is I've taken five strokes off my golf game."

> *Ellen DeGeneres, on coming out of*
> *the closet*

"The most intriguing game in the world played on the most beautiful playing fields of any sport."
Rhonda Glenn, golf commentator

"No one has ever conquered this game. One week out there and you are God. Next time out you are the Devil."
Juli Inkster

"Golf is a stupid game. You tee up this little ball. . . . Then you hit it, try to find it, hit it, and the goal is to get it into a little hole placed in a hard spot."
Juli Inkster

"Do your best—one shot at a time and then move on. Remember that golf is just a game."
Nancy Lopez

"This game is so crazy. You think you're playing well and you shoot a 75. You think you're going to miss the cut and you wind up shooting a 62."
Barb Mucha

"We want to develop our potential as human beings through the game of golf."

Pia Nilsson, director of the Swedish women's golf team

"You've got to do whatever it takes to get the ball in the hole. You have to take whatever shows up that day and make the best of it."

Ellen Port, amateur, on competing in some pro competitions

"Golf is entertainment. It has no relevance to world history."

Patty Sheehan

"It's a faithless love, but you hit four good shots and you started your day right."

Dinah Shore

"Adrenaline runs high, and you've got to find a way to control it. It's not like football or basketball."

Val Skinner

"When you're playing great, you can't wait for the next hole. But when you're playing lousy, you can't wait to get to 18 so the round will be over."
Hollis Stacy

"Golfers are like artists. If you don't have something to work with, you can't perform."
Hollis Stacy

"The old trite saying of 'one shot at a time' wasn't trite to me. I lived it."
Mickey Wright

"A never-ending challenge, frustrating but never dull, infuriating but satisfying."
Mickey Wright

"Golf is my means of expression."
Mickey Wright, on overcoming her innate shyness

GREAT DANE

"Yes, I've been the Danish champion three times, but that is nothing special."

> *Iben Tinning, on being Denmark's champ three times. There are only five professional women golfers in Denmark.*

GREAT ROUNDS

"It's always fun when you shoot a 67."

> *Amy Alcott, when asked if she had fun at a tournament*

"It's a good feeling to play a solid round. I'd love a chance to win or choke on Sunday."

> *Amy Alcott, on not winning in a long time*

"She should have lapped the field. In fact, she probably did lap the field."

> *Danielle Ammaccapane, on Vicki Fergon's round of 63 in a tournament*

"When I missed the 20-footer, my husband, my caddie, said, 'It's just as well you missed one. The fans were getting bored.'"

Donna Andrews, on settling for a par after six birdies

"I was in a zone. The holes were as big as bushel baskets."

Stephanie Farwig, after shooting a 64

"They just went in. I wish I knew why. If I did, I'd be about two million richer right now."

Jane Geddes, after shooting a 67

"I had to stay out of my own way."

Barb Mucha, after shooting a 62

"I had a good day at the office."

Penny Pulz, on her round of 69 in a tournament

"She got a ball and a hug."

> *Meg Mallon, on a shot of hers that*
> *hit a spectator and bounced back into*
> *the hole*

GREATNESS

"I can really say I'm one of the best. But if you have any modesty at all, it's tough to call yourself the best."

> *Nancy Lopez*

"I have to learn first to be number one. I check all the great players. I watch them—how they practice and rest. Everything comes quickly."

> *Se Ri Pak*

GREENS

"If this was Europe, these would be great greens."
Laura Davies, on players
complaining about the greens at
the Standard Register PING event

"The greens are so hard that you drop a ball and it bounces back in your pocket."
Rosie Jones, complaining about the
greens during a tournament

HAIL TO THE CHIEF

"When you're sitting there in a golf cart, it's like you're with any other player. . . . But then the round is over and the trucks and bulletproof cars roll up. All of a sudden, you know who you're playing with."
Amy Alcott, on playing golf with
President Clinton

"After all, I'm the Open champion, too."
> *Donna Caponi, after Orville Moody*
> *got a call from President Nixon*
> *congratulating him on winning the*
> *U.S. Open. Caponi never got a call*
> *from Nixon after she won the*
> *1970 Open.*

"Hey, Mr. President, how's Mamie's golf?"
> *Babe Didrikson, greeting*
> *President Eisenhower*

HAIR

"I think beards are repulsive. And I'd never date a man who has more hair than I do."
> *Donna Caponi*

"It is sort of like a Ph.D, but I have another life to lead."

> *Amy Alcott, on not qualifying for*
> *the Hall of Fame because she needed*
> *30 wins and she had been stuck on*
> *29 for many years, which was like*
> *pursuing a Ph.D.*

"My headstone will read, 'Here lies Amy Alcott, winner of 29 tour titles but not a member of the Hall of Fame.'"

> *Amy Alcott*

"If I win 30 tournaments and get picked up for ax murdering someday, I don't think I should be in it."

> *Amy Alcott, explaining why the Hall*
> *of Fame selection committee should*
> *focus on other things besides wins*

"If it doesn't happen, I'll go to my grave knowing that I was one of the best women golfers who ever lived."

Amy Alcott, on not being able to win her 30th tournament

"There were still people yelling at me, 'One more time, Amy.' I guess they hadn't heard the news yet."

Amy Alcott, after the Hall of Fame changed its guidelines, guaranteeing Alcott entry into the Hall of Fame

"I might not be a Hall of Famer in the record books, but I know I am in my heart."

Pat Bradley, before qualifying for the Hall of Fame

"To make it to most Hall of Fames, you either have to be retired for five years or six feet under."

Pat Bradley

"You need 30 wins to qualify for the Hall of Fame. It's important to me. Besides, it makes a good obituary."

JoAnne Carner

"When any of us get into the Hall of Fame, our name goes on a list and the LPGA throws a party. That's it."

>*Beth Daniel, downplaying the*
>*significance of the Hall of Fame*

"It would be lovely to do it, but we don't grow up with Hall of Fames in England."

>*Laura Davies*

"If I were to get in, I would like to have done it the hard way."

>*Laura Davies, on why she did not*
>*applaud new, less restrictive Hall of*
>*Fame guidelines*

"I have my Hall of Fame back at home with my kids."

>*Juli Inkster, on possibly not making*
>*the Hall of Fame*

"Do you want the Hall of Fame to have people in it?"

>*Juli Inkster, on the tough eligibility*
>*requirements of the Hall of Fame*

"How about Sunday night?"

> *Betsy King, leading in a tournament that would qualify her for the Hall of Fame if she won, asked by a press member if she would feel more comfortable having the discussion on Saturday night*

"If I don't think about it, then you guys [reporters] will remind me."

> *Betsy King, when asked if she often thought about the Hall of Fame since she was only one victory away from being eligible*

"There is an exact and exacting yardstick. Nobody gets in on a pass."

> *Jim Murray, on Hall of Fame eligibility criteria before they were changed*

"A woman's place may be in the Hall. But she'll have to crawl through barbed wire and shellfire and rocks before they'll let her in."

> *Jim Murray, on the Hall of Fame standards of the LPGA*

"My goal is the Hall of Fame. I'll do whatever it takes to get in there."

Dottie Pepper

"My hands were shaking on the last putt. The only problem with that is you never know which shake is going to hit the putter."

Patty Sheehan, on the win that would qualify her for the Hall of Fame

"If we don't change [requirements], then pretty soon there's going to be a bunch of old ladies in there, and then pretty soon those old ladies are going to die and then it's going to be the Dead Hall of Fame."

Patty Sheehan

"I would have to wait four more years, so I might as well wait to get the last one."

Annika Sorenstam, on losing a playoff that, had she won, would have given her enough tournament wins to qualify for the Hall of Fame. Under new eligibility guidelines, she would have to wait several years because of her age even if she had enough wins.

"When I started to play golf, I played it because I loved it so much, and suddenly you're achieving something like that. It's unreal."

> Annika Sorenstam, upon qualifying for the Hall of Fame

"No other person is involved in you getting in there. It's great."

> Kathy Whitworth, defending the 30-win policy of the LPGA Hall of Fame

"If you're going to do that, let's not call it the Hall of Fame, let's call it the Make Everybody Happy Club."

> Mickey Wright, on lowering the standards for entry into the Hall of Fame

HANDICAP

"I don't have any."

> Susie Maxwell Berning, three-time U.S. Open winner, when asked by a reporter who didn't know her what her handicap was

HATS

"When I don't play well, I blame my putting, not my hats."

> *Michelle McGann, recognizing the limitations of her lucky hats*

"I'd feel bad if I didn't play well and the hats were the only thing I was recognized for."

> *Michelle McGann, on her famous hats*

HEAVYWEIGHTS

"You don't knock Holyfield out unless you hit him over the head with a bat."

> *Laura Davies, playing in a Las Vegas tournament at the same time as the Lewis/Holyfield fight*

HEIGHT REPORT

"Tall men are hard to find. And most of them, peculiarly, go for short girls."

Carol Mann, 6'3", said in 1970

"It's tough when you can't see the player on the other side of the net."

Alison Nicholas, five feet tall, on why she gave up tennis for golf

HIGH SCHOOL

"Might have lost a few dates in high school."

Juli Inkster, on the drawbacks of being a major jock in high school

"They didn't like it very well that I beat them, but I didn't like to be beat either. I don't like to be beat at anything."

Michele Redman, on being a member of the boys' golf team in high school

"Detroit Red Wings."
> *Lorie Kane, Canadian pro,*
> *when asked to name her*
> *favorite hockey team*

"For me to win a major championship in Canada would be equivalent to how a Canadian hockey player would feel about winning the Stanley Cup for a Canadian team."
> *Lorie Kane*

HOLE-IN-ONE

"My first thought was, 'Wow, that makes the rest of the hole really easy for me.'"
> *Susie Redman, on her first*
> *hole-in-one*

"In my 57 years of golf, this hole-in-one is my first ever. To think how many balls I have hit in my life . . . I was running out of time."
> *Louise Suggs*

"I always dreamed of being a professional athlete. The WNBA wasn't around then, so I decided to pursue golf."

> *Sally Dee, All-American*
> *basketball player*

"In basketball, when I got angry I could play better. In golf, you can't do that. It's a game of rhythm and tempo."

> *Sally Dee*

"I own him now. It's probably good for a couple of laundries."

> *Wendy Ward, on her husband, Nate*
> *Hair, who left her during a*
> *tournament to see his alma mater,*
> *Gonzaga, play in the NCAA*
> *basketball tournament*

"It went out to pasture. It just wouldn't get out of the gate. It's totally opposite of me."

Amy Alcott, on her racehorse

"I've got three wins and three horses. That's one horse for every win."

Donna Andrews

"I was up all night, I was filthy, I was stinky, and I loved it."

Donna Andrews, on delivering a foal

HOTELS

"Anything clean."

Emilee Klein, offering her definition of a good hotel

INJURIES

"Heck, I may win this thing if it gets any worse."
> *Amy Alcott, on playing well while*
> *injured with a bad shoulder*

"I've had my share. A contact sport might have been easier."
> *Brandie Burton, on injuries she*
> *has suffered*

"I went out for a pass. It was a down and in, and I did a down and down."
> *Shirley Furlong, on how she injured*
> *her knee playing football with her*
> *family*

JULI INKSTER

"I'd want to be one shot in front of Juli on Sunday afternoon, because I think that will probably win."
> *Laura Davies, on the best way to win*
> *a tournament*

"If the LPGA was an army, they'd be saluting Juli Inskter as a major."

> *John Down, columnist,* Calgary Sun,
> *on Inkster winning all four majors*

"If we're coming down the fairway on the last hole, I love her to death, but I'm not going to give her the last putt."

> *Rosie Jones, on battling against*
> *Inkster over the lead in a tournament*
> *that would have qualified Inkster for*
> *the Hall of Fame had she won it*

"She's the kind of player who doesn't feel bad drilling it to you."

> *Dottie Pepper, on Juli Inkster's*
> *determination to win*

"I can hardly take care of myself. To do what she's done with having two kids, she's a superwoman."

> *Annika Sorenstam*

JEWELRY

"I got it a couple of years ago because I wanted to stand out when I went to the golf course."

Brook Lawrence, Texas Tech golfer, on wearing a nose ring

"I'm going to play the 14th hole 54 times. That's the only hole I want to play."

Terry-Jo Myers, on an event in which anyone who got a hole-in-one on the 14th hole won a million-dollar pearl necklace

JOBS

"You've got to have fun. Otherwise this would be too much like a real job."

Laura Davies

"If you can keep winning and enjoying it like I am, it's the best job in the world. It's not even a job, it's a hobby."

Laura Davies

"I really didn't want to go into the workforce, so I figured I would try the minitour."

Julie Larsen, on turning pro after graduating from college

"I'm very relaxed when I'm playing, because it's not a job, it's a game."

Nancy Lopez

"Maybe it's just that I hate having to work for a living."

Marilyn Lovander, on why she keeps bouncing in and out of the LPGA tour

"I would still like to do that [be an astronaut] if I could figure out a way to make my body younger."

Muffin Spencer-Devlin, on her life's ambition

"This is my job. What else am I going to do? I have all winter to do whatever else I want to do."

Sherri Steinhauer, on rarely missing a tournament

ROSIE JONES

"This is a woman with a personality and a shot. Both will go far."

Michael Madden, on Rosie Jones early in her career

LORIE KANE

"Everything has gone nicely south of the border, except trophy collecting."

Furman Bisher, on Canadian Lorie Kane, who constantly finishes second in tournaments and has yet to win

"The other caddies say she's the only player on the tour who smiles even after a bad shot. They want my job."

Danny Sharp, caddie for Lorie Kane

"I wish she'd stop being so nice and get some fire in her eyes."

Cathy Sherk, former LPGA player, on Kane never winning a tournament

CRISTIE KERR

"I don't mind losing to someone that good. It's like me playing tennis and losing to Steffi Graf."

> *Robert Floyd, top amateur player, on losing a match to Cristie Kerr*

BETSY KING

"The way Betsy was playing, Rin Tin Tin could carry her clubs and it wouldn't make any difference."

> *Gary Harrison, Betsy King's caddie, on a tournament in which she shot 17 under*

"All I can say is that our household was the only one where the father relinquished the sports section to the daughter."

> *Helen King, mother of Betsy, on Betsy's love of sports at an early age*

"The rap against women players is that they are inconsistent. Betsy is so consistent, it makes people sick."

Jim Murray

KONA COUNTRY CLUB

"The bunkers are a little like cat litter, but other than that, I like it a lot."

Janice Moodie, on the Kona Country Club in Hawaii

LAND DOWN UNDER

"People thought it's a nice dream to have, but you don't grow up in a small place like Ayr and become a professional golfer."

Robert Webb, Karrie's dad, on growing up in Ayr, Australia

LEADER

"Everybody is shooting at me and I have no one to shoot at."

Juli Inkster, on the disadvantage of leading a tournament

"I just don't feel comfortable leading the tournament. I'd rather be lurking. I'm lurking right now."

Muffin Spencer-Devlin, on being close to the lead in a tournament

LEADER BOARD

"The busiest person out there was the kid carrying our scorecard. He had to change my score every hole."

Janet Alex, on a round in which she had seven birdies and seven bogies

"This is like vuja de—never been there before."
Sally Dee, on being tied for first place after the second round of a tournament

"I've expended too much energy trying not to watch it."
Dana Dormann, LPGA pro, on trying not to watch the leader board

"I'll put blinders on."
Dale Eggeling, on not looking at the leader board while leading a tournament going into the final round

"Usually my friends start looking for me from the bottom up. Tomorrow, they will wonder why they can't find me."
Lori Garbacz, on leading a tournament after the first round

"That was a lucky coincidence. With a name that long, it helped that we didn't have to take all the letters down."

>*Don Kress, pressroom scorer, on*
>*Charlotta Sorenstam briefly taking*
>*the lead from sister Annika in a*
>*tournament*

"I get comfortable seeing my name on the leader board."

>*Kellie Kuehne, on leading a*
>*tournament early in her career*

"I was hoping [the leaders] were paying attention, but I was hoping they weren't getting inspired."

>*Meg Mallon, on coming from behind*
>*in a tournament*

"Dad will think it's a misprint."

>*Becky Pearson, LPGA pro, on being*
>*in second place in a tournament*
>*after three rounds*

"I never look at the leader board until late on Sunday if needed."

> *Lisa Walters, explaining why she did*
> *not know if she was leading a*
> *tournament*

"I'm just fascinated that I'm on it."

> *Lisa Walters, asked if she was*
> *surprised that no "big names" were*
> *on the leader board early in the*
> *LPGA Championship*

"I might not make enough birdies to win, but I'm there and they know I have the ability to make birdies."

> *Karrie Webb, when asked if*
> *opponents would be intimidated by*
> *her name being on the leader board*

LITERARY LIFE

"It's like being a writer. Unless you sell a story you're not going to make a cent."

> *Kate Golden, LPGA pro, on winning*
> *on the pro tour*

SALLY LITTLE

"I kept seeing her ass all day bending over to pick her ball out of the hole."

Hollis Stacy, on Sally Little shooting a final round 64 to win the Dinah Shore

LOOKS COULD KILL

"It's part of being a woman. We like men, too. Why does everybody like Freddy [Couples]? He's the best-looking guy out there. No one really cares how he plays. You just like to see his bum."

Helen Alfredsson, when asked if women should exploit their looks on the pro tour

"If I had legs like that, I'd pose that way too."

JoAnne Carner, defending Jan Stephenson's sexy poses in a golf magazine

"We would all like to look like Cindy Crawford, but we're professional golfers, not models."

Laura Davies, on the importance of looks on the LPGA tour

"Women's golf has never been marketed to showcase competence. It's been marketed to placate some of the traditional views of what women want to be—pretty, demure."

Carol Mann

"I think a lot of people come to watch us hit golf balls. But I'm sure that somebody enjoys watching someone who's attractive, too."

Liselotte Neumann

"It was good for the game, but it wasn't good for my golf game."

Jan Stephenson, on being used for her looks to sell golf

"Even though fashion and wearing makeup is important, it's still golf."

Jan Stephenson

"I'm just trying to make their lives easier. I'm not trying to change them into glamour girls."

Beverly Willey, salon owner who goes on the women's tour to help the players

NANCY LOPEZ

"Nancy with the smiling face."

Dave Andersen, columnist,
New York Times

"She was just 14, but they said she could already hit a ball farther than I could, and farther than a lot of other girls on the pro tour."

Jane Blalock, on Nancy Lopez

"If she uses only 75 percent of her talent, she could still win."

Donna Caponi

"People who have never played golf in their life, they know her name. That's a very rare thing."

JoAnne Carner

"She used to putt like it was easy. She made 25-footers as though they were 4-footers."

JoAnne Carner

"What's good for Nancy Lopez is great for the tour because purses will go up. Then it will be good for me because my salary will go up."

Frank Chilton, caddie on the
LPGA tour

"She was like God."

Beth Daniel, on Nancy's popularity

"You could tell a Nancy roar from someone else's roar."

Laura Davies

"Nancy just proves that golf is easy. Her father fixed fenders in the morning and taught her to play golf in the afternoon."

Herb Graffis

"Nancy Lopez never has an away game."

Betsy King, on the galleries' love
of Lopez

"Oh, I'm kind of used to that."
> *Sally Little, when asked how she felt*
> *about seeing Lopez's name on the*
> *leader board in a tournament*

"They say they've taken up a collection to send me on a three-week vacation."
> *Nancy Lopez, during her amazing*
> *win streak as a 21-year-old rookie*

"There might be some jealousies. But I would feel the same way if I was leading a tournament and all the reporters asked about Nancy Lopez. I can understand their resentment."
> *Nancy Lopez, on players being*
> *jealous of the attention given to her*

"You can't have more fun than playing golf with Nancy Lopez."
> *David Maher, chairman of*
> *a company, on playing in a*
> *pro-am with Lopez*

"There will never be another Nancy Lopez. They come along once in a century."
> *Meg Mallon*

"She plays by feel. All her senses come into play. That's when golf is an art."

Carol Mann

"She is like Arnie. She made it fresh . . . wholesome . . . warm . . . an OK thing to do and like."

Charlie Mechem, former LPGA commissioner

"It was worth being skulled just to meet her."

Dr. Jerry Mesolellar, after being hit by an errant Lopez shot

"People remember her always smiling, a friendly person, like a mom."

Se Ri Pak

"Other times when I go, I get many gifts. But this time, I went with Nancy, they forgot about me. She gets many gifts from people. I don't have any."

Se Ri Pak, on going back to Korea with Nancy Lopez

"Maybe I call her to say something, maybe I need some gifts or something."

> *Se Ri Pak, on the gifts Lopez*
> *received in Korea*

"Nancy Lopez was our Arnold Palmer."

> *Kathy Postlewait*

"They've got the wrong wonder woman on TV."

> *Judy Rankin, on Lopez, early in*
> *her career*

"Long after the great shots are forgotten, long after the victories blur into an amalgam of images, Nancy Lopez will be remembered for one indelible thing. That smile."

> *Ron Sirak, columnist,*
> Fort Worth Star

"I'm not given to ravin', but I don't mind ravin' about Nancy."

> *Mickey Wright*

"I feel good and I keep thinking I'm going to break out—but I keep killing myself before I start."

> *JoAnne Carner, at the beginning of her career*

"I keep losing."

> *Laura Davies, explaining why she was 1–8 in playoffs*

"I felt like I felt when I was playing basketball, when I was missing shots."

> *Lorie Kane, on how she felt after Canada lost a match-play tournament against the United States*

"Every day."

> *Patty Sheehan, on how often she thought about losing her big lead in the 1990 U.S. Open*

"How else could a girl travel all over the nation, meet so many interesting people, do the things she likes, and make lots of money?"

Donna Caponi, in 1971

"It hasn't been nearly as tough as Dad said. In fact, it's been a ball."

Donna Caponi, on her dad telling her the pro tour would be too hard

"We lead our own lives, doing what we love. We don't have to worry about doing the dishes or cleaning the house, and it certainly beats the eight-to-five office routine."

Kathy Whitworth, on her love of golf

LPGA

"Does that mean I now can drive from the women's tee?"

Bob Hope, after being made the first man in the LPGA

"If you want glamour, we've got that. If you want tough competition, we have that, too."
Meg Mallon, on the LPGA

"This was an organization suffering from a massive inferiority complex."
Charles Mechem, on the status of the LPGA in 1990

"Once a person is exposed to my girls, they become believers."
Charles Mechem, as LPGA commissioner

"Nothing ever hit me so completely. . . . Look at me, at 64, finally a feminist."
Charles Mechem, on the LPGA encountering discrimination

"If the LPGA was a stock listed on the stock market, I would be a major buyer."
Charles Mechem

"They all seem to have gone to Furman, and they all play the game like a cardplayer who keeps hoping for a pair of aces but keeps turning over treys."

Jim Murray, on the state of women's golf in the late '80s

"It fights long-term ingrained battles against the perceptions people have about women in sports."

Judy Rankin, on the LPGA tour

"If you can't find someone to love on the LPGA tour, you're not looking."

Jim Ritts, LPGA commissioner

"Fifty percent of the time you're a CEO, and 50 percent of the time you're an evangelist."

Jim Ritts, on his duties as LPGA commissioner

"If women's sports is the rising tide, then the LPGA is the biggest and longest-lasting ship in the ocean."

Ty Votaw, LPGA commissioner

"If the PGA tour is Coca-Cola, and the Senior PGA tour is Diet Coke . . . then the LPGA is Dr. Pepper."

Ty Votaw

MAJORS

"People make a big deal of the majors, so it's probably nicer to win them, because along with them comes more recognition, but personally a win is a win."

Laura Davies

"When I lay down my clubs, I could lay them down a lot easier if I had a major."

Rosie Jones

"My mother believes I'm getting more exposure now than when I won it."

Sandra Post, on holding the record for winning a major at age 20 until Tiger Woods and Se Ri Pak came along and won majors at younger ages

MALAPROPS AND
FRACTURED SYNTAX

"There are European players here from all over
the world."

Mary Bryan, LPGA TV commentator

"I think players and caddies need to have good
intercourse on a week like this."

Mary Bryan

"Nancy Lopez won five straight tournaments in
a row."

Charlie Jones

MEG MALLON

"If Mallon were any straighter, she'd be a ruler."

Thomas Bonk, columnist,
Los Angeles Times

"At first I was getting pressure from my family and friends about doing this. Now all my friends at the loan office are trying to figure out how they can get out here and caddie."

John Dormann, pro caddie for
Meg Mallon, on her success

"If you're looking for Meg, try the fairway. If she's not there, try the green."

Jim Murray, on Mallon's consistency

"She is as indefatigably cheerful as a guy selling insurance."

Jim Murray

"She even smiles when she three-putts."

Sonja Steptoe, reporter,
Sports Illustrated

"Oh no, except a few times when I'd like to putt for her."

> *Don Carner, when asked as an*
> *amateur golfer if he ever wanted*
> *to be out there in place of his wife,*
> *JoAnne*

"Jay doesn't fit on my stools, so we sit on the couch."

> *Kelli Kuehne, on having to change*
> *the furniture in her house since*
> *becoming engaged to pro football*
> *player Jay Humphrey*

"I'm a better loser than he is, and probably a better winner, because he rubs it in."

> *Nancy Lopez, on golfing with her*
> *husband, former major league*
> *baseball player Ray Knight*

"You know you've got to quit this life while you're young and not spend too much time thinking about getting married."

> *Carol Mann, said in 1968 to*
> *explain why she wanted to win at*
> *a young age*

"To get rid of my problems and my idiot husband."

> *Jan Stephenson, stating her goals*
> *for 1982. She later divorced her*
> *husband.*

M * A * S * H UNIT

"If I had known that by putting on a dress on a TV show I would have gotten an LPGA tournament named after me, I would have done it 50 years ago."

> *Jamie Farr*

"We need somebody with Annika and Karrie's results and Michelle's personality."

> *Danielle Ammaccapane, on the colorful hats and personality of Michelle McGann*

MEDIA WATCH

"If we were on TV every week, women's golf would be just as popular as men's, probably more."

> *Donna Caponi*

"I like the food and the locker room. There isn't a lot of privacy from the media in the locker room back home, but here there is."

> *Mi Hyun Kim, on the constant media attention in her homeland*

"Sometimes I want to stand in front of everybody and say, 'Hey, leave her alone.'"

> *Nancy Lopez, on the constant media attention given to Se Ri Pak*

"In Japan, I have no privacy. In the States, I can have a hole in my jeans and nobody will notice."
Ayako Okamoto

"Many media make me feel I must do my best golf. Many newspapers print my picture. I can feel it, but I don't want to think like that."
Se Ri Pak

"The people who hired me weren't interested in my perspective as a woman. They were looking for my perspective as a golfer."
Judy Rankin

"I'm glad they were there. I'm not usually in a position where the cameras are around me."
Angie Ridgeway, on being in contention in a tournament and having a camera following her shots

"I'm a recovering lawyer. One of those 12 steps is learning how to talk to the media."
Ty Votaw, LPGA commissioner

"Twenty years down the trek, people might be saying, 'Well, why aren't you more like Karrie Webb?'"

> *Karrie Webb, responding to critics*
> *who say she does not have a colorful*
> *personality*

MEN'S WORLD

"We're finally playing a course like the men play. Nobody complains when the men shoot low numbers."

> *Donna Andrews, on a course with*
> *consistently low scores*

"I'll play any woman golfer in the world even-up—and use only one club."

> *Julius Boros, at age 53*

"When you go out to a golf course, whether you're with men or women, you do feel like you're walking into a man's world."

> *Christine Brennan, columnist,*
> USA Today

"Golf is a man's world, and we're women trying to succeed in a man's world."
Beth Daniel

"The guys hit it so far that it's almost unreachable for the average person. Our game is more about tempo and rhythm. It's more natural."
Federica Dassu, Italian golf pro, arguing that the LPGA is good for the average golfer to watch

"If Faldo or Woosie [Ian Woosnam] or any of the boys had done what I have done, they would be Prime Minister by now."
Laura Davies, on the differences between men's and women's golf

"Our world is built on power. We don't have the power that men have. We never will. But we do play a great game."
Juli Inkster

"When we complain about conditions, we're just bitches. But when the men complain, people think, 'Well, it must really be hard.'"
Betsy King

"It used to be that men just came out here to gape at the women. They still gape, but they also come to watch us play now."
Sally Little

"People like to see players who are very feminine play like a man."
Nancy Lopez

"If a woman hits a ball into the rough, a man will say, 'Hit another one. We don't have time to look for a lost ball.' But if he hits a ball into the next county, he'll be looking in every gopher hole for it."
Alice Miller

"The hardest thing about women's golf is persuading the men to come and watch them."
Janice Moodie

"I like the fact that during LPGA events there is almost no chance that one of the players will suddenly light a cigar."
David Owen, columnist, Golf Digest

"Number one in the world."

Se Ri Pak, when asked if her goal is to be the number-one woman golfer in the world

"They think real life is playing golf all day on perfect golf courses for millions of dollars. . . . Real life is people, people who can't afford to eat."

Hollis Stacy, on men in the pro tour

"Guys have $200,000 and $300,000, $400,000 in the bank before they tee off. My backswing would be a lot looser if I had $300,000 or $400,000 in the bank before I teed off."

Hollis Stacy

"That was a hell of a long week for her, wasn't it? If she played five weeks in a row, she'd finish in the same spot."

Lee Trevino, on Laura Davies competing against men in a 72-hole event and finishing last

"The men's league does things in a more spectacular manner because increased power begets greater peril."

> Bob Verdi, columnist, Chicago Tribune, comparing the LPGA to the men's tour

"It's like the Mark McGwire/Sammy Sosa home-run race. People may have rooted for one player over the other, but what they did together helped grow the game."

> Ty Votaw, LPGA commissioner, comparing the LPGA and the men's tour

"We're not the powerful hitters men are, but we are smoother, and the duffer can learn as much watching us as the men."

> Kathy Whitworth

MENSA

"My game is not good but not bad."

> Se Ri Pak, at the halfway point of a tournament in which she was seven strokes behind the leader

"You have to make your mind take over, because after all these years, you've had millions of practice shots."

Amy Alcott

"You work so hard, you don't want anything to interfere. But then all of a sudden this little devil comes crawling out, saying, 'It's time to do something. You've been good too long.'"

Helen Alfredsson, on staying focused on tour

"I used to store my anger, and it affected my play. Now I get it out. I'm never rude to my playing partner. I'm very focused on the ball. Then it's over."

Helen Alfredsson

"The trouble with me is, I think too much. I always said you have to be dumb to play good golf."

JoAnne Carner

"Once you think about it, though, it's gone."
> *Beth Daniel, on getting nine birdies in a row*

"Golf is much harder. Tennis is all reaction. You have to think about things in golf."
> *Althea Gibson, champion tennis player and former pro golfer*

"Visualizing success is fine, but I can beat any 18-handicapper in the world. I don't care what their personal attitude is."
> *Betsy King*

"The mechanics part is more important than the mental part."
> *Betsy King, on playing well because of her swing*

"The game beats you up if you do, and I didn't want to get beat up."
> *Meg Mallon, on getting ahead of yourself*

"I'm a lot nicer to myself."

> *Michele Redman, on why she is playing better golf lately*

"I just play."

> *Patty Sheehan, when asked what technical aspects of her game she thinks about during a tournament*

"Get the goddamn thing in the hole."

> *Patty Sheehan, when asked what she was thinking about during a key putt in the 1992 U.S. Open*

"My golf game has always played havoc with my brain at night. Maybe I'll bring my cross to bed to fight those thoughts off."

> *Patty Sheehan*

"You don't need to miss a lot of putts to lose your confidence, but you need to make a lot of putts to get it back."

> *Annika Sorenstam*

"For some reason, I always play well when I use my brain."

Annika Sorenstam

"I tried every grip. It's not the grip. It's all between the ears."

Sherri Steinhauer, on her
putting problems

MIXED BAG

"It's stressful, but it's also relaxing. There's a lot of pressure because you worry about letting your partner down, but it's also fun to intermingle with all the guys."

Hollis Stacy, on playing in
mixed doubles

"I'm doing pretty well this year, but I'm pretty good at spending it, too."

> *Donna Andrews, on being second on the money list*

"A couple of good shots is the difference between staying in a Motel 6 and a Days Inn."

> *Michelle Bell, LPGA pro without a sponsor*

"I just heard my choking price."

> *JoAnne Carner, on a $4 million bonus being offered to any player who won several tournaments two years in a row*

"I'll enjoy the money, but I'm not so keen on making speeches or being on TV."

> *Laura Davies, on being a champion golfer*

"Oh well, it might have put me in another income-tax bracket."

Babe Didrikson, on not winning money in a tournament

"Money."

Nancy Lopez, asked to name the biggest changes in the game during her 20-year career

"If you thought about the money, you'd never be able to draw the club back."

Dottie Pepper, on the pressure of putting for $180,000

"I really did think it was maybe all the money in the world."

Sandra Post, on winning a major at age 20 and winning $3,000

"In too many sports, it's give me your wallet and get out of the way. That's not what you'll see on this tour."

Jim Ritts

"I like the thought of playing for money instead of silverware. I never did like to polish."

Patty Sheehan, on turning pro

"There is dysfunction within golf. The women are the last ones to get the money and the first ones to get the budget cuts."

Hollis Stacy

"You earned more than five times more money last year than I earned for my entire career."

Louise Suggs, to Karrie Webb

"He won the money and I won the money clip."

Louise Suggs, on playing in a mixed tournament with Ben Hogan

"My purses totaled less than $200,000. And if that doesn't make you want to throw up, I don't know what does."

Louise Suggs, on the early years of the LPGA tour

MOTIVATION

"I still want to beat the young girls."
> *Nancy Lopez, on what motivates her*
> *at age 42*

NAME GAME

"My dad just picked it. I don't know where he got it."
> *Grace Park, on moving to the*
> *United States and having her*
> *name changed to Grace from Jieun*

"I came out with little indentations in my head. My grandmother thought I looked like a muffin."
> *Muffin Spencer-Devlin*

"Looks like the Notre Dame backfield."
> *Sandra Spuzick, on being on the*
> *leader board with Silvia Bertolaccini*
> *and Joyce Kazmierski*

"It's too hard to pronounce, too hard to write, you always have to spell it to people, and everybody knows how to spell Walker."

> *Colleen Walker, on keeping her*
> *maiden name after marrying*
> *Ron Bakich*

NERVES

"A determined nervous, not a nervous nervous."

> *JoAnne Carner, when asked if she*
> *was nervous going into the final*
> *round of a tournament in which*
> *she was up by one stroke*

"A lot of nervous today. Like I almost puke."

> *Hiromi Kobayashi, on feeling nervous*
> *before a tournament*

"I know I'll have butterflies. I just want them to fly in formation."

> *Julie Larsen, on being two strokes off*
> *the lead going into the final round of*
> *the U.S. Open*

"Being nervous only gets you more in the right frame of mind for fear of failure."
Barb Mucha

"On the back nine, I felt like my nerves were swinging, not me."
Annika Sorenstam, on winning her first U.S. Open

"When you are playing well, your nerves are your friends. If I'm not comfortable with how I'm swinging and how I'm putting, that's when the nerves get in the way."
Sherri Steinhauer

LISELOTTE NEUMANN

"More personality in one afternoon than Bjorn Borg, Stephan Edberg, and Mats Wilander have in their careers—all combined."
Thomas Boswell, on the outgoing personality of Swedish golf star Liselotte Neumann

NUMBERS GAME

"I love numbers. Any kind of numbers."

*Annika Sorenstam, on her fascination
with numbers and using her computer
to calculate the number of putts in
each hole*

OAKMONT

"You just have to keep hitting the ball as solid as
you can, because this course isn't going to accept
anything less."

Jane Geddes, on Oakmont

"It's so easy to get on the bogey train out there."

*Juli Inkster, on the distances of
Oakmont*

OH, CANADA

"You start the season in corduroy and turtlenecks
and end it in corduroys and turtlenecks."

Gail Graham, on golf in Canada

AYAKO OKAMOTO

"She's a combination of Princess Di and Sadaharu
Oh."

Jim Murray, on Ayako Okamoto

OLD WAVERLY

"I think the women like that. There's not any billy-
goat action."

*Bob Cupp, designer of Old Waverly in
Mississippi, on the course's lack of
huge hills*

"Personally, I'd rather see birdies than bogeys."
> *Juli Inkster, on grumbling because of low scores at Old Waverly*

SE RI PAK

"There's times when people ask if she's upset with me because we don't talk and she walks alone on the course a lot. But it's because she's so focused all the time."
> *Jeff Cable, Se Ri Pak's caddie*

"She's young and nerveless, and that is an unbeatable combination."
> *Laura Davies, on Se Ri*

"With Se Ri, you just count the holes until she catches you."
> *Laura Davies*

"She's the best news South Korea has had this year."
> *Lee Hong-Koo, South Korean ambassador to the United States, on Se Ri*

"Most players are in their late 20s or 30s before they find a formula for handling the pressure. Se Ri loves the pressure."

David Leadbetter, her former coach

"Shot after shot, she's so much better than anybody right now."

Nancy Lopez, in 1998, on Se Ri

"Se Ri is a great little player. Great mind, aggressive, not afraid of anything."

Nancy Lopez

"She may mean more to the Korean people than Jordan means to America."

Tim McNulty, LPGA official

"No, not yet, but good start."

Se Ri Pak, when asked if she was the best player in the world after winning back-to-back majors

"She definitely has a lot to learn, but she's obviously an A student."

Dottie Pepper, on Se Ri Pak's rookie year

"She seems to be one of those athletes who transcend her sport."
> *Jim Ritts*

"Pak did the golf equivalent of reading *War and Peace* in 30 minutes."
> *Ed Sherman, columnist,* Chicago Tribune, *on Se Ri learning to play golf in only two years*

GRACE PARK

"She drives off the tee better than she drives a car."
> *Tom Friend, sportswriter,* New York Times, *on Grace Park at age 16*

"I thought it was her driver. Then I looked and she was using the same driver I was, so that couldn't be the reason."
> *Sherri Steinhauer, on Grace Park's 276-yard driving average*

"I thought she hit a sprinkler head."

Wendy Ward, on Grace Park almost driving a ball 300 yards

PENALTIES

"I asked if I was getting a two-stroke penalty for being ugly, and she said, 'No, we're stopping play.'"

Amy Alcott, on a Tour official telling her she had some bad news

DOTTIE PEPPER

"If I could pick one player for our team [Solheim Cup], it would be Dottie because she's such a competitor."

Helen Alfredsson

"It doesn't matter to Dottie. She puts enough pressure on herself. It doesn't matter if one or ten people are charging after her."

> *Donna Andrews, when asked if she thought that it bothered Dottie Pepper that six players were one stroke behind her going into the final round of a tournament*

"If there's one person I'd want to have make a putt for me, it's Dottie."

> *Juli Inkster*

"I thought I was playing pretty good golf, and I lost by what, six."

> *Meg Mallon, on Dottie Pepper winning the Dinah Shore*

"If she were a guy, she'd be someone like Michael Jordan. She'd be that popular."

> *Judy Rankin, on Dottie Pepper*

PHILOSOPHY

"Hitch up my girdle and let it rip."
Amy Alcott, her golf philosophy

"I defy the ball not to go in the hole."
Amy Alcott

"Hit the ball and go find it again."
Laura Davies, her golf philosophy

"We want to make the impossible possible. To find answers, we have to ask questions as if the impossible was possible."
Kjell Enhager, sports psychologist for the Swedish women's golf team

"If all the golf courses in the world closed down tomorrow, I wouldn't drop dead."
Juli Inkster, on outside interests

"I don't ever say die. I wouldn't have lasted this many years out here if I didn't have that characteristic in my personality."
Rosie Jones

"Being in professional golf, everybody sees you for your performance. But you are someone who performs, you are not a performance."

Pia Nilsson, Swedish national coach

"If you don't shoot a low score, you behave as if your whole life is a bad score."

Annika Sorenstam, on the American philosophy of golf

"I would think my life would be so limited and so shallow if all that interested me were birdies and bogies."

Muffin Spencer-Devlin

PLANES, TRAINS, AND AUTOMOBILES

"I called my mom and told her to go and buy a new Mazda."

Amy Alcott, on splitting the $500,000 purse in a mixed-team tournament sponsored by Mazda

"Maybe I lost it on the plane."

> *Helen Alfredsson, after playing well for a time and then doing poorly in a tournament*

"It's a little odd checking on flights out of town on Friday."

> *JoAnne Carner, on missing her first U.S. Open cut in 25 years*

"It's not a bad life if you don't mind living out of a suitcase."

> *Kathy Cornelius*

"I did it in Germany. I wouldn't admit to it anywhere else."

> *Laura Davies, on driving 181 mph in her Ferrari*

"But I can't seem to get anything. I seem to get stiffed by all the airline companies."

> *Laura Davies, on being involved in five different frequent-flyer programs*

"A spectator said, 'I don't think you understand. You have to hit the hole, not the car.'"

> *Mary Dwyer, after hitting the car that would be awarded to any player who hit a hole-in-one during a tournament*

"After being that nervous, being behind the wheel of a 725-horsepower car, that putt didn't seem so bad."

> *Dale Eggeling, on drag racing and winning a tournament within one week*

"I've never had a woman pilot come to me and say, 'I think I'll just learn on my husband's old B-29 until I get better, then I'll try a Cessna.'"

> *Betty Hicks, on being a golf teacher and a pilot*

"I hope to win more of these and start my own dealership."

> *Sally Little, on her second year in a row winning a tournament that awarded a Mazda to the winner*

"Lucky her. I got to use my old car."

Federica Dassu, on Annika
Sorenstam coming to a tournament
in a new jet

"One very close to the airport."

Annika Sorenstam, on where in
Florida she wanted a second house

"I don't think the police really need to know what speed we did."

Karrie Webb, on driving at high
speeds in Laura Davies's Ferrari

"Whistle, what whistle? I didn't hear a thing."

Joyce Wethered, on a train going
by while she was preparing for
an important putt

"When she missed her par putt, I said 'This is my bread and butter.' I don't miss three- and four-footers."

> *Rosie Jones, after winning a playoff against Becky Iverson*

"We're the same age [20]. It would look like we were friends. Like we play a practice round."

> *Se Ri Pak, on her and Jenny Chuasiriporn having a playoff to determine the 1998 U.S. Open champion*

"I had a tiger by the tail and there wasn't very much I could do about it."

> *Kathy Whitworth, on Sandra Post, at age 20, beating her in a playoff to win a major tournament*

POCONO MANOR COURSE

"It would be a good course to have an affair on. Once you get in the trees off the fairway, no one will find you."

Amy Alcott

POTTY TRAINING

"If I'm playing good, I'm not going to go. I'll put my rain pants on if I have to."

Dale Eggeling, on her refusal to go to the bathroom during a tournament

PRACTICE

"You don't gain much by practicing off every fairway."

JoAnne Carner, on practicing shots in the rough

"You just turn up and hope you are playing well. This stuff about getting ready is a lot of rubbish."

Laura Davies, on getting ready for a tournament

"Never practice without a thought in mind."

Nancy Lopez

"I do practice hard, but after a few hours, I get so bored."

Grace Park

PREGNANT PAUSE

"I hope so, but a ballerina would be fine, too."

Dawn Coe-Jones, six months pregnant, when asked if her child would take up golf

"I have backed off a couple of shots out there—gotten a jolt."

Dawn Coe-Jones, describing being six months pregnant and having the baby kick her

"I've heard that pregnancy makes you play better. Your center of gravity is lower, and you stay down through the shot a little better."

Tammie Green

"That putt was so good, I could feel the baby applaud."

Donna Horton-White, on hitting a 25-footer while she was seven months pregnant

"My husband brought a catcher's mitt in case he had to catch the baby."

Sarah Lebrun Ingram, on playing in a tournament while she was seven months pregnant

"The two of them will do fine. I hope our 13th person gives us an advantage."

Judy Rankin, on picking the six-months pregnant Tammie Green for the Solheim Cup team

"I always wondered what one of these things looked like."

> *Marilyn Lovander, during a press conference at the press tent during a tournament in which she held the lead*

"I didn't even know where the press tent was."

> *Sandra Palmer, on leading a tournament after not winning in three years*

"Hope to see you guys tomorrow or, even better, on Sunday."

> *Kelly Robbins, talking to the press after leading in the second round of a tournament*

PRESSURE

"I used to think pressure was standing on a four-foot putt knowing I had to make it. I learned that real pressure was 65 people waiting for their food with only 30 minutes left on their lunch break."

Amy Alcott, on being a waitress early in her career

"Having a three-shot lead, everyone would expect you to win. But with a one-shot lead, it's anybody's win, so I guess there is a little pressure."

Laura Davies

"I don't throw up."

Sandra Haynie, when asked to describe the major difference in her golf game over the last 20 years

"I don't know pressure."

Se Ri Pak

PUMPKIN RIDGE

"I should think if you're four or five under Sunday morning, you're going to have a very good squeak at it."

> *Laura Davies, on Pumpkin Ridge Golf Club in Oregon, home of the 1997 U.S. Open*

PUTTS

"It looked as long as Long Island or Rhode Island."
> *Amy Alcott, on a 35-foot birdie putt*

"God knew I couldn't putt, so he put me close to the hole."

> *Barbara Barrow, after making five birdies in the last nine holes of a tournament*

"Every putt *can* go in, but I don't *expect* every putt to go in."

> *Jane Blalock*

"I think it's the most boring thing in the world to practice."

Jill Briles-Hilton, on her short game

"My putter has been very nice to me the last three days. I just need it to hold on for 18 more holes."

Brandie Burton, on leading the du Maurier Classic after three rounds

"That's fine, but I hit my putts as long as my driver."

Laura Davies, on being the longest hitter on tour

"If it's my day, they go in, and on a bad day, they won't."

Laura Davies, on her putting

"I have a disease of leaving it short. It's not the putter, it's the golf gods."

Jane Geddes, on her putter

"It all depends on my putter. I can tell you some great stories about my putter and some very sad ones."

Janice Gibson, on being three strokes back of the leader going into the final day of a tournament

"Sometimes I had too much speed, and other times, not enough. But this is golf—I cannot be perfect all the time."

Se Ri Pak, on her putting

"Maybe it was that cup of coffee I had this morning."

Hollis Stacy, on missing four putts, each under eight feet

"When my putting is on, I'm usually around the top 10. When it is not, I'm fighting to make the cut."

Sherri Steinhauer

"The people in Pittsburgh were giggling and pointing out the grip. But the putts were going in."

Dave Stockton, on winning a Senior Tour event with a putter borrowed from Donna Caponi, that had a blue and yellow grip

"Because they go in."

Karrie Webb, when asked why she switched to a cross-handed putting style

"The hole started to look as big as a bucket. If I knocked it 15 feet, it was like a gimme putt."

Karrie Webb, after a good stretch in a tournament

"I've been fortunate to be blessed with good health and the ability to make a lot of putts."

Kathy Whitworth

"Judy's like someone who puts on a big party and wants everybody to be happy when they leave."

>*Rosie Jones, on the style of Judy Rankin as Solheim Cup coach*

"She is so small, she might get lost in an unreplaced divot."

>*Bob Toski, on Judy Rankin*

RECORDS

"I'm not a very good history buff when it comes to golf. I just thought it would be cool to shoot a 9-under."

>*Kelli Kuehne, on missing the U.S. Open first-round record by one shot*

"They don't let women play there much, so hopefully it will stand for a while."

>*Mhairi McKay, on setting a women's record of 67 for the St. Andrews Old Course*

"Unfortunately, I don't pay a lot of attention to stuff like that. But for those who do, they'll see my name."

> *Kelly Robbins, on setting the LPGA record for a 72-hole score with 265*

"I certainly didn't make history the way I played."

> *Caryn Wilson, the first person since Althea Gibson to play in both the golf and tennis U.S. Opens, after shooting an 80 in the golf event*

RELIGION

"My dad wasn't sure, but as long as it didn't affect my golf game, it was fine."

> *Kathy Baker, on finding religion*

"Not even close . . . but it was a pretty good second."

> *Alison Nicholas, when asked if winning the U.S. Open was the best thing that ever happened to her, even more important than her deeply held religious beliefs*

REPEAT PERFORMANCE

"I think it's the biggest advantage you can have.
You've got better memories than anyone in the
field."

>*Karrie Webb, on defending a title*

RETIREMENT

"I cannot find a job that pays me $700,000 a year,
so until I do, I'll be right here."

>*Pat Bradley, when asked if she
>would retire after entering the
>Hall of Fame*

"I told the younger players I'll continue until they
start to beat me."

>*Pat Bradley, on when she
>would retire*

"I'm not going to ever think about it until I shoot my address. I live at 30-30 South Ocean Boulevard."

> *JoAnne Carner, when asked if she was going to retire at age 60*

"As long as I am improving, I will go on, and besides, there's too much money in the business to quit."

> *Babe Didrikson, when asked, after she had won virtually every golf tournament, if she would retire*

"I'm making the longest farewell tour since the Grateful Dead."

> *Charlie Mechem, on retiring as LPGA commissioner*

"I'm tired of taking the family on the road to watch me play bad golf."

> *Patti Rizzo, on retiring at age 39*

"Quitting a sport is like quitting cigarettes. It ain't easy."

> *Mickey Wright, on retiring from golf*

"He means well. . . . He's always in a hurry. He always has to go do this and that."

*Helen Alfredsson, on LPGA
commissioner Jim Ritts*

RIVALRIES

"When we're both going well and playing head to head, I don't play for second."

*JoAnne Carner, on her rivalry with
Nancy Lopez*

"Karrie doesn't have a rivalry with anyone right now. . . . If somebody else is finishing second every week, then maybe you have a rivalry, but no one is doing that right now."

*Laura Davies, on the supposed
rivalry between Karrie Webb and
Annika Sorenstam*

"She was taught to play the golf course, not some individual."

> *David Esch, husband of Annika*
> *Sorenstam, on her rivalry with*
> *Karrie Webb*

"I still haven't forgiven Rosie for that."

> *Tammie Green, on Rosie Jones*
> *hitting a 50-foot putt in a playoff*
> *to beat Green*

"I kind of want to trip her as she goes by."

> *Nancy Lopez, on Alison Nicholas, two*
> *years after Nicholas beat her in the*
> *U.S. Open*

"She's such a fly at a picnic. She just won't go away."

> *Dottie Pepper, on her rivalry with*
> *Danielle Ammaccapane*

"To be the best, I have to beat the best."

> *Annika Sorenstam, on her rivalry*
> *with Karrie Webb*

"We want to beat each other because that's who's leading the golf tournament."

> *Karrie Webb, on her rivalry with*
> *Annika Sorenstam*

KELLY ROBBINS

"She was a good kid. I never had to spank her."

> *Cindy Figg-Currier, on LPGA pro*
> *Kelly Robbins, whom Figg-Currier*
> *once baby-sat*

"I don't think she wants to come off as somebody who bet the farm and lost. The fact is, she has the talent to bet the farm."

> *Judy Rankin, on the laid-back*
> *approach of Kelly Robbins*

ROBOT

"When I stand over the ball, something clicks in and I become a machine."

> *Nancy Lopez*

ROCKY

"I don't want to take any of his money."
> *Kris Tschetter, on playing a practice*
> *round with Sylvester Stallone*

ROLE MODELS

"I wanted to be Sam Snead."
> *Amy Alcott, on who she wanted to be*
> *growing up*

"Before I was in my teens, I knew exactly what I wanted to be: I wanted to be the best athlete who ever lived."
> *Babe Didrikson*

"I want to be Nancy Lopez, Betsy King. . . . They are the best players, but really nice to people."
> *Se Ri Pak*

"They put the rookies out there at 5 A.M."
> *Kellee Booth, on her biggest*
> *frustration as a rookie*

"They come out and they win, and they win fast and they win a lot."
> *Laura Davies, on rookies*

"Ten years ago, rookies were rookies. They were afraid to mix it with the big names. Now the big names are afraid to mix it with the rookies."
> *Laura Davies*

"I have 14 clubs and they have 14 clubs. Now let's see who can get some putts to drop."
> *Dorothy Delasin, LPGA rookie,*
> *describing her attitude toward*
> *players on the Tour*

"It was so long ago, I think I was still sucking my thumb."
> *Nancy Lopez, on the 20th*
> *anniversary of her being named*
> *Rookie of the Year*

ROYALTY

"She didn't ask about the backswing."

> *Laura Davies, when asked if she got*
> *any advice from the Queen*

"There's more pressure than a three-footer on Sunday, I can tell you."

> *Laura Davies, on having the Queen*
> *put a medal on her*

RULES

"I don't claim to know the rules. That's why we have a field staff."

> *Danielle Ammaccapane, after*
> *breaking a rule*

"You have to play by the rules of golf, just as you have to live by the rules of life. There's no other way."

> *Babe Didrikson*

SAND TRAP

"I stayed in the bunker until I made one. They had to bring me cocktails and dinner."

> *JoAnne Carner, on how she got to be*
> *a good bunker player*

SECOND PLACE

"I don't even think about first place. The IRS takes all of it anyway."

> *Laura Baugh, on her frequent*
> *second-place finishes*

"It's around the corner. I just don't know what corner."

> *Lorie Kane, on always finishing*
> *second*

"I don't know, but if you can tell me, I'll show up."

> *Lorie Kane, when asked what she*
> *will tell her fans after she gets her*
> *first victory*

"I would rather chase, as long as I can chase from fairly close. Let someone else have a restless night and answer questions about how to maintain a lead."

Dottie Pepper

"Paybacks are hell."

*Dottie Pepper, a year after winning
the Nabisco by 6 strokes, she finished
second by 10 strokes*

SENIOR TOUR

"What ticks me off is seeing how much the seniors are making playing on Mickey Mouse golf courses, shooting 20 under par."

*Helen Alfredsson, on the men's
Senior Tour*

"All of a sudden we're there. . . . It's like making five birdies in a row."

*Jane Blalock, on the creation of the
women's Senior Tour*

"You can call us the 40-somethings."
> *Jane Blalock, proposing a name for*
> *the women's Senior Tour*

"They can't be considered senior golfers, but they're no longer running in Se Ri's pack."
> *Gary D'Amato,* Milwaukee Journal,
> *on the women's Senior Tour*

"What would you rather watch—talented and pretty girls, or a bunch of men over the age of 50?"
> *Helen Wadsworth, European tour pro,*
> *on the Senior Tour*

PATTY SHEEHAN

"There's no such thing as the 'best' golf swing. Sheehan's just looks like it ought to be."
> *Tom Boswell,* Washington Post

"To watch Patty Sheehan swing a golf club is to witness the gift of natural grace."
> *Jaime Diaz,* Sports Illustrated

"The best sign of how good Patty is, is that she hasn't changed putters during her career."
Meg Mallon

"She probably has the best golf swing on any tour since the young Gene Littler."
Jim Murray, on Patty Sheehan

DINAH SHORE

"We may never take another nonplayer into the Hall of Fame, but if we only take one, it should be Dinah."
Nancy Lopez, on Dinah Shore being inducted into the LPGA Hall of Fame

"Dinah had so many friends, it helped the tour turn the corner. It stands apart from anything else in women's golf."
Judy Rankin

"As a golfer, I make a colossal singer."
Dinah Shore

"I haven't been able to sleep for a couple of nights thinking about it."

> *Dinah Shore, on jumping into the*
> *water with Amy Alcott after Alcott's*
> *second win in the Dinah Shore*

"She had a song for every shot. If the ball rimmed around the cup, she would start singing 'Around the World in 80 Days.'"

> *Kathleen Sullivan, on Dinah Shore*

DINAH SHORE NABISCO CHAMPIONSHIP

"Other than the U.S. Open, and that's because of the tradition, this is the tournament most of the players want to win. It's the tournament I wanted to win."

> *Amy Alcott*

"Nobody knows that I've won this tournament, but they know I've jumped into the water."

> *Amy Alcott*

"I wanted to accept the trophy with dignity, but I guess that's just not my style."

> *Amy Alcott, on jumping into the*
> *water after winning the Dinah Shore*
> *for the first time*

"I'd really do something wild. I'll have to think about what it could be, but I promise I'll keep my clothes on."

> *Amy Alcott, asked what she would do*
> *if she won her fourth Dinah Shore,*
> *after jumping into the water after*
> *winning her first three*

"It's too soon to know what this winning means, but I got a shock when I hit that cold water."

> *Donna Andrews, on the significance*
> *of winning the Dinah Shore*

"Nabisco makes cookies. Change it to the Dinah Shore."

> *Walter Bingham, columnist,*
> Sports Illustrated, *on calling it*
> *the Nabisco Tournament instead*
> *of the Dinah Shore*

"It was a Fortune 500 corporation. The other events were more like chamber of commerce events."

> *Jane Blalock, comparing the*
> *Dinah Shore with other events*

"The other tournaments were tournaments. This was an event."

> *Jane Blalock*

"The tour was still Podunk when we went to Palm Springs for the first time, and suddenly we were celebrities."

> *Jane Blalock, on the impact of the*
> *Dinah Shore*

"I'm going to keep knocking on that door until someone lets me in."

> *Pat Bradley, on always coming close*
> *but never winning the Dinah Shore*

"I went to the Masters, and when I saw the scoreboard, I thought 'That's what this is to the men.'"

> *Pat Hurst, on the impact of the*
> *Dinah Shore*

"I don't know how to swim."

Pat Hurst, leading going into the
final round of the Dinah Shore,
when asked if she would jump into
the water if she won

"That was peer pressure. I wasn't going to get in over my head when I don't know how to swim."

Pat Hurst, on her brief walk in the
water after winning the Dinah Shore

"I didn't jump in. I am kind of a klutz, and I could have sprained an ankle or something."

Betsy King, on walking into the
water after winning the Dinah Shore

"I guess going into the lake is better than the champagne bath I took in Atlantic City. That champagne stank worse than the lake."

Betsy King, on walking into the
water after winning the Dinah Shore

"I think the most embarrassing thing would be to have one of the Generation X-ers coming up and asking who Dinah Shore was."

> *Dottie Pepper, happy that the name was changed from the Dinah Shore Classic to the Nabisco Classic*

"I always dreamed of winning the Dinah Shore with a birdie putt. I never thought I'd win the Dinah Shore by two-putting from 126 feet."

> *Patty Sheehan*

"I was very dignified, was I not?"

> *Patty Sheehan, after wading into the water following her Dinah Shore win*

"I didn't dive. I didn't jump. I very discreetly walked in."

> *Patty Sheehan, on that same bath*

"Alcott's Alley."

> *Dinah Shore, proposing a nickname for her tournament after Amy Alcott won it three times*

"People call me the garbage queen."
*Lauri Merten, on her strong
short game*

SHOTS HEARD 'ROUND
THE WORLD

"Crummy."
*Lynn Adams, LPGA pro, when asked
to describe the shots she hit to
two-putt from 15 feet*

"You know, oh good, I'm in the trees. Anyone else
would be madder than a house."
*JoAnne Carner, on her fascination
with tough shots*

"No, I think I have much to learn about my golf
game. I hit stupid shots many times."
*Se Ri Pak, when asked if she was
one of the top players*

SIBLING RIVALRY

"My brother quit playing for 20 years because I could outdrive him."

JoAnne Carner

"I had to pick and shove my way up to the table to get some food."

*Rosie Jones, on her competitive
nature being spurred on by being
one of eight children*

SKIING

"I don't go fast enough."

*Danielle Ammaccapane, downplaying
fears she would break her leg because
of her love of skiing*

SLOW PLAY

"I was just trying to make a statement."

Lori Garbacz, after criticizing slow play by ordering a pizza that arrived before she got into the clubhouse

SLUMPS

"It hasn't been up and down. It's pretty much down all the way."

Danielle Ammaccapane, on her slump from 1993 to 1996

"All I did was apply a little polish to a Rolls-Royce."

Ted Yossuf, mentor of Dottie Pepper, on advising her through a slump

SOCCER

"It's a sisterhood. There's such a charm and exuberance about these girls. I was just in awe of them."

> *Betty Jameson, Hall of Fame golfer,*
> *on what the U.S. soccer team meant*
> *to women's sports*

"If Mia had six months to work on her golf game, she would be a scratch golfer. That is how great an athlete she is."

> *Meg Mallon, on playing golf with*
> *Mia Hamm*

SOLHEIM CUP

"Myself, of course. We'd be rockin' and rollin'."
> *Helen Alfredsson, when asked who*
> *should captain the European Solheim*
> *Cup team in 2000*

"The Ryder Cup with lipstick."
> *Anonymous*

"To make history and to start history, that's an honor."

Pat Bradley, on participating in the first Solheim Cup competition in 1990

"Rooter. I am going to get some pom-poms and just get out there."

JoAnne Carner, on the role she saw for herself as the Solheim Cup captain in 1994

"We're friends with everyone on the opposing side—until this week."

JoAnne Carner, on the rivalry flamed by the Solheim Cup competition

"I've got a headache and I'm ready for a Stoli."

JoAnne Carner, on her first day as Solheim Cup captain

"What would be better than wiping the smiles off the American faces? They think they are going to beat us again. I think otherwise."

Laura Davies, said before 1992 Solheim Cup

"I can be a hero or I can not be a hero, but either way, when this is over, I'm still gonna be Tammie."

> *Tammie Green, on the significant role envisioned for her on the 1998 Solheim Cup team*

"When we get here, we're the best of friends, and when we leave, we're not."

> *Rosie Jones, joking about the Solheim Cup rivalry*

"I wanted the twelve best players from Europe, whether they were all from Spain or all from Stockholm."

> *Pia Nilsson, Swedish coach and captain of the Solheim Cup team, after coming under criticism for picking six of her twelve players from Sweden*

"I'll iron. I'll sew. I'll caddie. They are wonderful players, and I want to give them a chance to play their best game."

> *Judy Rankin, explaining her strategy as Solheim Cup captain*

"I told her it was like buying a thoroughbred racehorse. Take the one that's running the best."
Yippy Rankin, husband of Judy, on how to select members of the Solheim Cup team

"They had to choose between one of us grayheads."
Patty Sheehan, on her and Pat Bradley being contenders for the Solheim Cup captaincy

ANNIKA SORENSTAM

"Losing to Annika Sorenstam has been compared to getting your butt kicked by Miss Manners."
Anonymous

"As a player, I have to step it up to a different level when she's ahead."
Pat Hurst

"She's grossly great."
Juli Inkster

"It is like a shark developing a better appetite."
> *Ferd Lewis, Honolulu advertiser, on*
> *Sorenstam losing her confidence and*
> *than gaining it back*

"For Annika, I don't think anything is impossible."
> *Liselotte Neumann*

"If this promoter-crazed world was a banana split—
Annika Sorenstam would be the scoop of vanilla."
> *Dan O'Neill, St. Louis Post Dispatch,*
> *on her easygoing personality*

"A baby-faced assassin."
> *Jim Ritts*

"I think every course sets up for Annika."
> *Kelly Robbins, when asked if a*
> *specific course set up for Sorenstam*

"If I were a comedian, I'd be on VH-1."
> *Annika Sorenstam, on her quiet*
> *personality*

"I kept thinking to myself, 'What golf course is she playing?' It didn't look to me like she was playing the same course."

Kris Tschetter, on Sorenstam winning the U.S. Open by six strokes

"It is special to win against someone who inevitably will be the best player to ever play the game."
Karrie Webb

"She's Miss Consistency. She doesn't miss fairways."
Karrie Webb

MUFFIN SPENCER-DEVLIN

"She hasn't had a career, she's had an Italian opera."

Anonymous, on Spencer-Devlin's coming out of the closet and also spending time in a psychiatric facility along with various other activities over the years

SPIRO IS MY HERO

"I think a woman would have the patience to cure his slice. He needs help from someone."

> *Shirley Englehorn, LPGA player, on the terrible golf game of former vice president Spiro Agnew*

HOLLIS STACY

"She was Tiger Woods before Tiger Woods was Tiger Woods."

> *Rhonda Glenn, USGA director of communications, on U.S. Girls champion and three-time U.S. Open champion Hollis Stacy*

SHERRI STEINHAUER

"She attacks the golf tour each year like she has been locked inside a Wisconsin ice rink all winter."
Melissa Isaacson, in the Chicago Tribune, *on Steinhauer's love of the game*

JAN STEPHENSON

"I wish someone had asked me to pose."
JoAnne Carner, asked how she felt about the furor surrounding the seminude pictures taken of Jan Stephenson in Fairway *magazine*

"I watched Jan's stroke and almost suffered one myself."
Bob Hope, on the attractiveness of Stephenson

"I sometimes think my life has been a little like a soap opera, but Jan had moments that are right out of *General Hospital*."

Nancy Lopez

"She makes the tour an afternoon soap. Any way you look at it, it's good theater."

Jim Murray, on the career of Jan Stephenson

"I thought she was just a pinup. Now that I know her record, I'm much more impressed."

Karrie Webb, on fellow Australian Jan Stephenson

MARLENE STEWART-STREET

"If Marlene ever turned pro, she'd need a Brinks truck following her around each week."

JoAnne Carner, on the legendary amateur star Marlene Stewart-Street

"Physically, you need an oxygen tank after a few holes."

Colleen Walker, on the hills at Stoneridge Country Club in San Diego

STREAKS

"I view golf as an art. I've been missing a few colors."

Amy Alcott, during a losing streak

"When you're shooting a good score, you don't even know what you're doing. It wasn't that hard."

Helen Alfredsson, after one of her winning streaks

"You take it when you get it, and right now I'm gettin' it."

Beth Daniel, during a hot streak

"I can't afford not to play, the way I've been playing."

> *Beth Daniel, on her refusal to take a break during a winning streak*

"It looked like I was putting into a big bucket."

> *Juli Inkster, after putting well to win a tournament*

"The game seems very, very simple almost. The holes look big, the fairways wide, and you can't do anything wrong."

> *Nancy Lopez, on hot streaks*

"I don't want streaks. I want a Hall of Fame speech one day. Careers aren't built on streaks."

> *Dottie Pepper*

"It got to the point where my swing was good enough that I felt I could not shoot a bad round. It was a feeling that stayed with me for four years."

> *Mickey Wright, on winning 35 tournaments in a four-year period*

"I don't think Hogan or Nicklaus was ever criticized for demanding excellence for themselves, so why should I be?"
Dottie Pepper, on her critics

"Enjoy the successes that you have, and don't be hard on yourself when you don't do well."
Patty Sheehan

"My success was totally up to me. I didn't do it for the galleries or money. Playing well was self-gratifying."
Kathy Whitworth

LOUISE SUGGS

"Her name isn't Miss Suggs. It's Miss Slugs."
Bob Hope, on Louise Suggs hitting a huge drive during a pro-am tournament

SUNGLASSES

"When I was winning this tournament in 1986, we didn't have sunglasses to hide behind. . . . Cover them up [your eyes], and no one knows if you're happy, sad, nervous, or scared."

Pat Bradley, on the difference sunglasses have made to golfers in the late '90s

SUPERSTITIONS

"I've got my lucky fishhook on, my lucky coins, and I'm wearing my favorite colors."

Katie Peterson-Parker, on playing in a tournament on Friday the 13th

"I just keep away, I hide behind trees, anything so Hollis won't see me. She and I are superstitious."

Tillie Stacy, Hollis's mom, on rooting her daughter on during tournaments

SWEDISH INVASION

"The guys in the clubhouse thought the Swedish bikini team was coming."

> *Carin Hjalmarsson, on the*
> *unorthodox techniques of the*
> *Swedish women's golf team*
> *practicing in Naples, Florida*

"She was one of the first to come to America, and when she tells us her stories about adjusting to a new country, it makes us feel better knowing she was even stupider than we are."

> *Annika Sorenstam, on Pia Nilsson,*
> *the Swedish women's golf coach*

SWIMMERS

"Put a swimming pool in my backyard."

> *Amy Alcott, after winning $90,000 in*
> *the Dinah Shore Classic and jumping*
> *into the water, when asked what she*
> *would do*

"Finish high and let 'em fly."
> *Patty Berg*

"With some of the players, I spend a lot of time looking at the clovers because I don't want to watch their swings."
> *JoAnne Carner, on not being impressed with the swings of some players*

"I've got a flat, quick, ugly swing, but I've saved a lot of money on lessons."
> *Dawn Coe-Jones*

"My swing is no uglier than Arnold Palmer's, and it's the same ugly swing every time."
> *Nancy Lopez*

"I don't think they argue with me now."
> *Annika Sorenstam, on childhood coaches telling her to keep her head down when she swung, advice she disagreed with*

"No matter how powerful your engine, you must have gradual acceleration of speed. So it is in a golf swing."

Mickey Wright

TALK TOO MUCH

"I'm a talker if I'm playing with talkers, or I'm not a talker if I'm not with talkers."

Karrie Webb

TAX MAN

"In Spain, we pay 60 percent taxes and can't get anyone to pick up the garbage."

Marta Figueras-Dotti, taking issue with men on a pro golf tour complaining about high taxes

"I said I was retired but I couldn't pass up the chance to see my parents. Plus it's a tax write-off."

Lenore Rittenhouse, on visiting her parents while playing in a tournament in her home state of Hawaii

TEMPER, TEMPER

"My original dream was to play golf well enough to be allowed to throw my clubs."

JoAnne Carner

"I've always been even-tempered, fun-loving, and all the rest. But it turned out, when I hit a golf club, I turned into a tyrant."

Jane Geddes

"I broke the bottom of more golf bags faster than I could buy them."

Jane Geddes, on her temper

TIGER TAILS

"The crowds have been bigger at our tournaments this year. I noted a lot more younger people around the 18th green. I can only assume that it's because they think golf is cooler."

Laura Davies, on the influence of
Tiger Woods on women's golf

"Tiger has left me some privacy."

Karrie Webb, on her phenomenal
success being overshadowed by
that of Tiger Woods

TOUGH SHOTS

"I'd rather have an 8-iron from the rough than a 4-iron from the fairway."

JoAnne Carner, on her love of
difficult shots

TRAVEL PLANS

"You have to wake up somewhere in the world. So what difference does it make where you are?"

> *Laura Davies, denying that travel affects her play*

UNUSUAL SHOTS

"I'll take a two-shot penalty, but I'll be damned if I'm going to play the ball where it lies."

> *Elaine Johnson, on a tee shot that landed in her bra*

"You should have walked out and dropped it into the green."

> *Mardi Lunn, LPGA pro, to a spectator after the ball she hit landed in the spectator's pocket*

"This is big country with many big players, many strong people. This is where I need to be."

Se Ri Pak, on the importance of playing in the United States

U.S. OPEN

"Even if you pretend it's not, there's no getting around that this tournament is special. You feel emotions this week that you don't get any other week."

Helen Alfredsson

"I'll probably sleep on it, think about it, and get nervous."

Jill Briles-Hinton, on her first-round lead in the U.S. Open

"I did something by climbing over 113 golfers. But there were 114 ahead of me, weren't there?"

JoAnne Carner, on finishing second in the U.S. Open after a first-round 81

"I wish it could have been a 54-hole tournament—the last 54."

JoAnne Carner, on that same first-round 81

"Nancy Lopez didn't lose the Open to Alison Nicholas. She just didn't win it."

Gary D'Amato, Milwaukee Journal, *on dramatic '97 U.S. Open win by Alison Nicholas over Nancy Lopez*

"A win."

Dale Eggeling, when asked what would make the 20th year different after going 0-for-19 in previous U.S. Opens

"Playing in the Open is like driving to the Hamptons for the weekend and getting stuck on the Long Island Expressway—a beautiful journey ruined."

Lori Garbacz

"That week we had an earthquake, we had a train wreck, a chemical spill, and we had a plane crash . . . so we were busy. That was survival of the person who didn't have to get evacuated the most."

Jane Geddes, on the 1986 U.S. Open

"Of course we're here. This is the Open."

Brian Inkster, Juli's husband, on reporters being surprised to see so many husbands at the Open

"This is the U.S. Open. Par is a prized possession, birdie is like a bonus, and bogey is to be expected."

Kelli Kuehne, on the U.S. Open

"I spent the whole day worrying about whether someone would see my underwear."

Nancy Lopez, after finishing second in the U.S. Open and blaming her loss on a broken zipper

"I don't feel like I have to win the Open, but more than anything I'd love to win the Open."

Nancy Lopez, on never winning the U.S. Open

"What Alison did out there was unbelievable. That has to rank with what anyone—male or female—has ever achieved in the U.S. Open."

> *Nancy Lopez, after Alison Nicholas won the 1997 U.S. Open*

"I need two Valiums, quick."

> *Nancy Lopez, after two of her group shot nine and six on one hole in the 1998 U.S. Open*

"I've won the Open and I've lost the Open. Winning it was the hardest thing I've ever done."

> *Meg Mallon*

"The USGA is smiling. Their idea of a perfect U.S. Open is to shoot even par and win."

> *Meg Mallon, on only three players being under par after three rounds of the 1995 U.S. Open*

"You don't really win an Open, you sort of hang around and survive it."

> *Barry McDermott*, Sports Illustrated

"I kept telling myself this is the Indianapolis Open. I didn't want to say it was the U.S. Open."

Lauri Merten, on mental techniques she used to win the U.S. Open

"I'll probably schedule my flight out for Friday night, as I usually do."

Terry-Jo Myers, on playing in the U.S. Open

"I'm sure Old Waverly is nice, but I'm not going to bring my family to the Open and make them stay at a Super 8 Motel."

Terry-Jo Myers, on the U.S. Open being held at Old Waverly in a small town in Mississippi

"If Nick Faldo or Colin Montgomerie had won the men's U.S. Open, I guess it would have been front page news. Because my victory was in the women's U.S. Open, I stayed on the back pages."

Alison Nicholas, on how the British papers portrayed her U.S. Open victory

"Nancy has always offered me her support, though I don't know about that right now."

> *Alison Nicholas, on having a*
> *three-shot lead over Lopez going*
> *into the final round of the U.S. Open*

"Yes, and getting more and more, too."

> *Se Ri Pak, when asked after winning*
> *the U.S. Open if she was the most*
> *famous athlete in Korea*

"The Open requires getting your brain into action, as opposed to most weeks."

> *Dottie Pepper*

"The thing you have to learn is not to throw away the candy store."

> *Patty Sheehan, on her heartbreaking*
> *loss at the U.S. Open to Betsy King*
> *before coming back a few years later*
> *to win the Open*

"As a kid, I played tennis. I used to dream of winning the U.S. Open, but in tennis."

> *Annika Sorenstam, on winning the*
> *golf U.S. Open*

"Those blue blazers don't scare me. I know the people inside those blue blazers."

> *Hollis Stacy, on not being intimidated by USGA officials who were wearing blue blazers in the U.S. Open*

"There's really no secret. If it's your week, it's your week, you know."

> *Hollis Stacy, when asked her secret in winning three U.S. Opens*

"Each one was like a different baby."

> *Hollis Stacy, when asked which of her three U.S. Open victories meant the most*

"My gosh, 29 in a row. I'm exhausted. Can I take a nap now?"

> *Hollis Stacy, on tying the record of playing in 29 U.S. Opens in a row*

"This one seems easy. But I'm sure after the USGA gets done, it will be brutal."

> *Jan Stephenson, after playing a one-day tournament at the Merit Club in Illinois, home of the 2000 U.S. Open*

"It is seriously to be doubted if any woman golfer has ever played a stretch of 36 holes with the power, accuracy, and overall command."

Herbert Warren Wind, on Mickey
Wright's win at the 1961 U.S. Open

VACATION

"Party all night, sleep all day, nonstop eating."

Se Ri Pak, on her plans for the
off-season

"Clean my house. Sit on my couch."

Kris Tschetter, on what she would do
during a four-week break at the end
of the season

VIDEOS

"Is that the X-rated one called 'Swingin' in the Nude'?"

*Amy Alcott, when asked if she
planned a new version of her
instructional video*

VOCAL CORDS

"What do you expect? I've been yelling at the golf
balls all week."

*JoAnne Carner, on losing her voice
after a tough tournament*

WEATHER WATCH

"After Nashville, can New Jersey be as bad? Never.
Just a little walk in the sun."

*Amy Alcott, on players complaining
about 90-degree weather in
New Jersey*

"Give me heavy, rough, tight fairways, wind, rain, hail, you know, and I might set a course record."

Amy Alcott, on being a notoriously good player in bad weather

"You could basically wear your whole suitcase."

Helen Alfredsson, on a tournament where the weather went from warm and sunny to cold and rainy

"I needed night goggles out there."

Beth Daniel, on playing in the dark due to a rain delay

"I'd rather be a wet rat than a cold-handed rat. Once my hands get cold, I'm done, so I'd rather my hands be warm and my hair look like whatever."

Laura Davies, on playing in the rain with no umbrella

"Birdies don't matter, pars matter."

Laura Davies, on being happy making par in bad weather

"I'm voting for rain delays."
> *Judy Dickinson, on coming out after a long rain delay and scoring two birdies and an eagle*

"We pretty much carry along everything week to week—from shorts to winter clothes."
> *Ellie Gibson, LPGA pro, on being prepared for all weather*

"It really throws my makeup off. I've got to keep reapplying."
> *Juli Inkster, joking about the effects of the heat during the U.S. Open*

"It was a perfectly normal English day."
> *Trish Johnson, tour pro from Great Britain, on a miserable rainy day*

"I grew up on an island. I'll be happy."
> *Lorie Kane, on predictions of strong winds before a tournament*

"She was more scared than when she saw *Poltergeist II*."

> *Margie Kato, interpreter for Ayako Okamoto, on Okamoto seeking shelter during a terrible rainstorm*

"I learned many things. This is golf. It's up and down."

> *Se Ri Pak, on shooting 77 in a wind storm*

"I'd much rather play a different golf course in different conditions. It definitely takes a lot of field out of it."

> *Dottie Pepper, on the miserable weather conditions at a golf course*

"It puts you in a different mind-set. It puts you in a birdie mode instead of trying to grind for pars."

> *Dottie Pepper, on rain delays that softened the greens and fairways*

"I didn't feel a thing. I was numb."

Yippy Rankin, husband of Judy, on watching his wife play in the Dinah Shore while he was wearing short sleeves despite a 30-degree temperature change

"This is Edinburgh, but it's more like Scotland than the USA."

Val Skinner, on the miserable weather conditions for an Edinburgh, Minnesota, golf tournament

"I felt like the Michelin Man out there most of the day."

Muffin Spencer-Devlin, after a bitterly cold day

"I do rather like the wind. I like to think I was born in a tempest."

Muffin Spencer-Devlin, on playing well in the wind

"You have to hit a lot of different kinds of shots. It's fun to play in, because you need an imagination."

> *Sherri Steinhauer, on playing in gusty winds*

"I never worried about bogey—which is rare for me, I might add. It's usually birdies, bogeys for me."

> *Kris Tschetter, on good weather conditions in a tournament that is known for miserable conditions*

"I got a couple of workouts in."

> *Karen Weiss, who strength-trains in the off-season by shoveling snow in Minnesota*

"I needed hip boots instead of golf shoes."

> *Shelly Wendels, LPGA pro, on playing a course that had just received 15 inches of rain*

"We can't play out here. It's hailing."

> *Kathy Whitworth, urging officials to stop play in a 1985 tournament*

"When Karrie gets on a roll, there's no stopping her from making a lot of birdies. All you can do is just get out of the way."

Donna Andrews

"She's definitely the best woman ball-striker I've ever seen."

Ian Baker-Finch

"That's good for the rest of us. It might give us a chance to win."

Jane Crafter, on Karrie Webb taking a four-week hiatus

"She made me feel like a hack. That's how good she is."

Beth Daniel

"It wouldn't make a bloody bit of difference. I would just get bored."

Laura Davies, when asked if practice would help her beat Karrie Webb

"Trying to catch Webbie is a massive incentive. Everyone else seems to be chucking their hand in, but I'm keeping my hand out there."
Laura Davies

"She has the swing, the head, and the hunger to dominate the game as no woman has since Mickey Wright."
Jaime Diaz, Sports Illustrated

"She reminds me of me."
Steve Elkington

"Can you believe that little devil? I believe she is the best ball-striker in the world right now."
Jane Geddes

"Her bad shots are better than 90 percent of players' good shots."
Jane Geddes

"To beat her, you have to play flawless golf because she plays flawless golf."
Rachel Hetherington

"She has raised the bar, and now there's like a new level that you've got to work to get to almost."

Rachel Hetherington

"Karrie doesn't just want to win, she wants to beat you."

Juli Inkster

"Considering her domination, they might start calling her Tigress."

Kevin Iole, Las Vegas Journal

"She doesn't see where she can hit it, she sees only where she's going to hit it."

Lorie Kane

"Karrie is at that level now that I don't think anyone else can get to."

Lorie Kane

"In any sport."

Carol Mann, when asked if Karrie Webb had the best rookie year in the history of women's golf

"We all love it when she skips an event."
Cindy McCurdy

"If she continues at this rate, she'll retire as the greatest woman player ever."
Jack Newton, television commentator

"You can change the year, but you can't change the story."
Dottie Pepper, on Karrie Webb starting where she left off and beginning the year with a tournament win

"I get inspired playing with her. It inspires me to see someone hit a good shot every hole."
Annika Sorenstam

"I wish I had her on the President's Cup team. She'd give the men something to think about."
Peter Thompson

"Joyce Wethered was a great golfer, for she hit the ball as far as the average scratch player and with feminine grace."

> *Henry Cotton, on the top female*
> *player of the '20s and '30s*

"I have no hesitancy in saying that, accounting for the unavoidable handicap of a woman's lesser physical strength, she is the finest golfer I have ever seen."

> *Bobby Jones, on Wethered*

"She is the greatest striker of the ball, regardless of sex."

> *Gene Sarazen, on Wethered*

"Joyce was the most finished player I ever saw. She could have played on the men's tour, she was that good."

> *Gene Sarazen*

"When she had to putt, she got it every time."
> *Sandra Haynie, on the great putting*
> *of Whitworth*

"She is the best under pressure of anybody who ever played on the tour."
> *Carol Mann*

WILDLIFE

"I felt like a shark out there. Out here, I felt like a little fish."
> *Nancy Bowen, on being a star of*
> *the Futures Tour and not winning*
> *as a pro*

"I'm not going to get my gander up. That's a goose, isn't it? They get mad. That's what I need, something to get me going."
> *Patty Sheehan, on being more*
> *aggressive*

"Obviously, he wasn't going spikeless."

> *Hollis Stacy, on having to wait at*
> *a hole because a deer print had to*
> *be fixed*

"I had never heard that sound in my life. . . .
I thought it was a cow."

> *Karrie Webb, on being interrupted by*
> *the croaking of a frog*

WINNING

"Concentrate, play your game, and don't be afraid
to win."

> *Amy Alcott, on the keys to winning*

"You can't be scared to win. When you win, you let
yourself win."

> *Amy Alcott*

"You just fall into it. It's like getting the last seat
in the movie theater. You just get lucky."

> *Amy Alcott, on winning*

"How crappy can you play and still win? It came down to perseverance."

> *Helen Alfredsson, on winning a*
> *tournament despite a lousy last round*

"Victory number 31."

> *Pat Bradley, asked what challenges*
> *lie ahead after qualifying for the*
> *Hall of Fame after winning*
> *tournament number 30*

"This is one of the few times I've been close enough to think about winning. So tell Hollis I'd like a very nice present from her."

> *JoAnne Carner, four strokes behind*
> *Hollis Stacy in the second round of*
> *the Dinah Shore*

"Relax. You're getting too far ahead."

> *JoAnne Carner, advice to playing*
> *partner Juli Inkster, who had a four-*
> *stroke lead going into the final two*
> *holes of the Dinah Shore*

"I could accept failure, but I could never except quitting."

> *Betsy Cullen, on winning her first tournament after her eighth year on tour*

"Everyone on their week can win a tournament, but there's about a dozen that can win every week."

> *Laura Davies*

"I was always a bridesmaid. I just couldn't catch the bouquet."

> *Stephanie Farwig, at age 39, on her LPGA career*

"Not to hit bogey."

> *Akiko Fukushima, when asked the key to winning a tournament*

"I guess I'm just a slow learner."

> *Carolyn Hill, on her first win after 15 years on tour*

"I don't have to play my best game to win. I think I have to think the best and grind the best."

Juli Inkster

"I don't get to win as much as the really great players, so when it comes, you just have to really enjoy it."

Rosie Jones

"Winning never gets old."

Nancy Lopez, when asked if she ever got tired of winning

"The winners are the ones who are thinking the best, using their minds the best."

Nancy Lopez

"Nobody ever remembers who finishes second."

Nancy Lopez, on her determination to win

"Great champions have an enormous sense of pride. The people who excel are those who are driven to show the world and prove to themselves just how good they are."

Nancy Lopez

"If I knew what it was, I'd take it with me every week."

Meg Mallon, when asked her secret after winning her third Sara Lee Classic

"I'm not too happy with the way I'm hitting the ball. I haven't hit it solid."

Alice Miller, after winning a tournament by eight shots

"Somebody told me I can lose but keep the money. I don't want the money. I want the trophy."

Se Ri Pak, on the U.S. Open playoff against amateur Jenny Chuasiriporn. Even if Pak lost she would get the first-prize money.

"I like to think I was a little less neurotic than some about winning."

Betsy Rawls

"Tomorrow, if it's meant to be, I'll shoot one less than everybody else."

Kelly Robbins, tied for the lead going into the last round of a tournament

"Someone is going to have to play well, and I have to play bad."

Annika Sorenstam, on how she could lose a tournament

"If I watched it on TV, I would have been in awe of the person doing that."

Karrie Webb, on making four birdies in the last five holes to win the du Maurier classic

"Am I conscious? I don't feel like it out there."

Karrie Webb, on her third-round 67 to take an eight-shot lead in the Nabisco Championship

"It was pretty bloody hard. It's not the prettiest golf I ever played."

Karrie Webb, coming from behind to win the Australian Ladies' Masters

WOMEN

"If you are too rough, you're wrong. If you're not, then you're wishy-washy."

Helen Alfredsson, on the way women athletes are perceived

"Golf has many traditions, not the least of which is to treat women as second-class citizens."

Christine Brennan, USA Today

"It's OK for women to perspire. I still like flowers. I still like to have the door held open for me."

Juli Inkster

WONGLUEKIET SISTERS

"The tour is lucky that they can't be out here for another five years. We can make some money before both of them are out here."

Karrie Webb, on the future greatness of the 13-year-old Wongluekiet sisters

"Conditions on the other tours can be brutal. The weather is harsh, the travel is inconvenient, the courses are inconsistent, and the money is bad."

Amy Alcott, on foreign tours

"You become more spoiled when you come here. . . . The courses are so much better. When we go back home, we kind of laugh at the differences."

Helen Alfredsson, on differences between the U.S. and European courses

"I suppose this is a case of women's inhumanity to man."

Joe Flanagan, on being fired as the director of the Women's European Tour

WRIGHT AID

"Some pretty good golfers on the course . . . and they all have breasts, as far as I know."

> *Laura Davies, on golf commentator Ben Wright's remarks that women golfers are handicapped because they have breasts*

"How does he know? He doesn't have any."

> *Nancy Lopez, on Wright's comments about breasts handicapping women golfers*

MICKEY WRIGHT

"I didn't think anybody but the Babe could hit 'em like that."

> *Babe Didrikson, on the swing of 19-year-old Mickey Wright*

"If Mickey Wright was playing at the peak of her career today, she'd win, but she wouldn't dominate."

Betsy King, said in 1995

"Mickey Wright was the best female player ever, bar none. And there's not even a second, third, fourth."

Dave Marr

"Mickey got the outside world to take a second look at women golfers, and when they looked they saw the rest of us."

Judy Rankin

"She had the right combination of mechanically sound swing and enormous personal drive."

Betsy Rawls, on Wright

"Mickey had a better golf swing, hit the ball better, could play rings around Babe."

Betsy Rawls, comparing Wright to Babe Didrikson

"She set a standard of shotmaking that will probably never be equaled."
Betsy Rawls

"She was just head and shoulders above everyone."
Kathy Whitworth

WYKAGYL

"It's probably my favorite course to play because if you're not playing well, you won't score well."
Beth Daniel, on Wykagyl in Westchester, New York

"If you can win here, you can win anywhere."
Tammie Green, on Wykagyl

INDEX

Italicized page numbers indicate names referred to in a quote. All other names are actual sources of a quote.

243